GET YOUR HAIR CUT!
YOU 'ORRIBLE LITTLE MAN!

Michael R. Kettle

First published in Great Britain in 2003

ISBN 0-9545051-0-7

Edited by Anne Bradford

Designed and typeset by The Studio Publishing Services Ltd, 4A Brookside Units, Venny Bridge, Exeter EX4 8JN

Printed by Bookcraft, Westfield Trading Estate, Midsomer Norton, Bath BA3 4BS

Published by Fernhill Books, 23 The Cedars, Fernhill Heath, Worcester WR3 8RU.

Tel: 01905 452440.

E-mail: michael.kettle@btopenworld.com

Contents

Biographies

Mike Kettle lives just north of Worcester and has two daughters and three grandchildren. He is retired, and spends his busy life writing books (this is his fourth), giving talks and working on a shared allotment. He is also the editor of the magazine of the Worcester/ Birmingham Canal Society, *The Fifty Eight*, and a committee member of the same society.

Anne Bradford is married with three adult children and one grandson. She has written and published ten books of ghost stories, *A History of Stourport on Severn*, and is currently about to publish *A History of Redditch*. She is a member of several historic and local interest societies, and is involved in displays and exhibitions too numerous to mention.

This book is dedicated to all my former colleagues in the Royal Armoured Corps, especially those who loaned photographs, added their recollections, and made me realise my memory was not as great as I had imagined! I am grateful to all who have assisted with photographs and given their time to help bring this project to fruition.

Introduction

I would imagine there can be no ex-serviceman who is not familiar with that phrase, or indeed the complete version of it. NCO stands close behind the recruit and bellows in his ear 'Am I hurting you? I should be, I'm standing on your hair! Get your hair cut, you 'orrible little man!' It is one of a number of things that someone who completed National Service could never forget.

During the 1940s, 1950s and 1960s, many thousands of British young men were drafted into one or other of the armed services to complete a period of National Service. During wartime, there was no specified duration, and those men were regarded as regular forces and demobilised as soon as possible after the war ended. Thereafter, those drafted into regular units were expected to serve for eighteen months. They could be posted anywhere in the world they were needed, to the home units, or to trouble spots. Most were eighteen years of age, although some were deferred until later, due to special reasons. The length of service was later extended to two years, and during the height of the 'cold war', some found their engagement stretching to two and a half years.

This is the story of one National Serviceman who completed two years' service, mainly at Catterick Camp in Yorkshire, in the Royal Armoured Corps. Fifty years later, I recall some of the traumas, adventures, and humour of that experience. No doubt many readers will be able to identify with some of these happenings, both painful and pleasurable to the memory.

Michael R. Kettle 2003

Chapter One

Called for Duty

I drove the family saloon up the hill, and into the yard at Kidderminster station, where, even at 7.00 a.m. there was a group of taxis and a Midland Red bus from town, disgorging its small load. To enter the station one had to walk beneath an ornate canopy into the black and white Victorian building. My Dad and I strolled unhurriedly to the booking office where my travel warrant was exchanged for a single ticket to Richmond Yorkshire, a place I had previously only heard of. A small queue of people had formed at the barrier for their tickets to be checked, and we joined on the end before passing through to the platform.

A mere few minutes later, a steam engine hissed and wheezed along the whitened edging stones, dragging behind it a tender full of coal, and four or five seemingly reluctant coaches. The whole ensemble clanked to a halt, the engine issuing forth a great blast of steam. Several passengers alighted, and it was time for me to board. Stopping only to hug Dad, and check that I had my small suitcase in my hand, I entered the compartment and found a seat by the window which was already running with condensation. The engine whistled, let out another cloud of steam, and began to heave the load towards Birmingham. We waved to each other before Dad moved back towards the station entrance, and I left on a journey into the unknown.

Ever since leaving school at the age of sixteen and a half I had been aware that any career I chose would inevitably be interrupted by this military service. The Korean war was at its peak and the length of service required had recently been extended from eighteen months to two years much to the chagrin of those who were waiting for their call-up. In my case, the extra time would only be a little more inconvenient, since the career suggested by my parents, in the stationery trade could easily be put on hold. I had wanted to go into the Metropolitan Police, but owing to my being too young, even for cadets, I allowed myself to be talked into the family business, after first serving a brief apprenticeship in a nearby town at a well-known stationers Mark and Moody. It was the first of many instances where I took what seemed to be the easiest way, resulting in life-long regrets. But that is another story.

Anyway, here I was on my way to serve my country as a soldier.

The story had really begun just prior to my eighteenth birthday when I was required to register at the local Ministry of Labour, followed soon afterwards by visits to Birmingham and Worcester for questions, tests and a medical examination. I cannot recall which part took place at which centre but I had to visit both units.

With regard to my choice of arm, having spent time in two lots of Army cadets, both at school and later, there was never going to be an alternative to choosing the Army. Also, I had no wings so I could not fly, thus the RAF was a non-starter, and although I could swim, I disliked the sea, so the Royal Navy was never in the running. I did, however, hope that I might be accepted for the Royal Engineers, for I had always held an interest in maps, and I was told the RE was the unit for such things. My given choice was the first example of never volunteering, because in the end, you just do as you are ordered.

So far as the medical was concerned, as long as you had two of everything you should have two of, the matter of passing was a foregone conclusion. When it came to checking one's private parts, apart from the embarrassment, little did I think that years later, the great comedian Ken Dodd would include a sketch in his 'Laughter' show where the medical officer commented on the small size of those parts. Ken's great laugh line was 'We're only going to fight them, aren't we sir?' Their tests were quite thorough, and they decided that everything was in working order. I could have told them that I had not yet had a chance to test everything out, so even I could not be sure the more vital parts of my equipment were in proper working order. However, it was a comfort to learn I had perfect vision, and no flat feet or fallen arches.

My natural desire was 'Let's get on with it', so that the sooner I went in, the sooner I would be out again. Things do not work that way; my impatience had to be curbed, and until they were ready for me I had to wait.

Our postman became used to seeing me at our gate, and my asking if he had THE envelope yet. I must have been a right pain in the *derrière*, and I do not know who was most pleased when the brown OHMS package finally arrived, the postman, my parents, or me.

The charade of asking me what branch of the Army I wished to join was now revealed for what it was, because I discovered that I had been placed in the Royal Armoured Corps. The reason for this did not become obvious to me until I finished my service, at which time I found out that the local Territorial Army the Queen's Own Worcestershire Hussars was a Cavalry unit attached to the RAC.

My instruction said I was to report to the 65th Training Regiment, Royal Armoured Corps, Catterick Camp on Thursday 19th March 1953, enclosed a rail warrant, a list of what to take and what not to take, and so here I was on the way.

The carriage was warm, steamy and full of cigarette smoke. I used to smoke in those days, so there was not the complaint I would have made today, since learning the health dangers of passive and active smoking. There was comfort to be obtained from this fuggy atmosphere, and smoking was allowed on trains. Fifty years on, I would have had a window open before you could say 'Players please.'

Leaving home held no terrors for me, or so I thought, having boarded at school for the final year and a half, but I suspect Mum did not want to say farewell in public, and consequently did not travel with us to the station. Although school had been a mere three miles down the road, I was hardly out of contact with home; nevertheless I felt that I would be able to handle this new parting. I had received plenty of advice on how to behave from well meaning family and friends, although it seemed to me that I should behave properly at home as well as away. My upbringing was such that I would never let the family down, despite the occasional desire for kicking over the traces..

My girl-friend, who lived far away in Scotland, had wished me well both by letter and telephone, but as we lived so far apart and seldom saw each other, this new life was hardly likely to make a difference to our relationship, a first for both of us, and still very much in the early stages.

More than an hour and numerous stations later, the train arrived at Birmingham's Snow Hill station from where a walk across the city to the other main line station, New Street, was necessary in order to catch the connection to the North East. There was plenty of time to spare as we had planned the departure from home to give sufficient time for catching the next train going to York, Darlington and beyond. Only something catastrophic or totally unavoidable could prevent me from catching the connection from New Street, and thus failing to report to the final destination on time.

In the 1950s, New Street was entered through a main entrance hall in Navigation Street, from where a long bridge crossed over all platforms. Stairs led down onto the platforms from both sides of that bridge, and there was a smaller rear entry from Station Street also connected with the bridge. Most platforms had their own waiting rooms, buffets and book stalls.

There was no shortage of directions to the correct platform, but it would have been difficult to have missed the one from which the train would depart: on looking down from the bridge one could see little knots of young men, either standing or walking around, each with a small suitcase looking decidedly nervous and anxious. Perhaps one of the best descriptions would be 'like cats on hot bricks'.

Once down with the others, I found that the conversations were invariably centred around what regiment we were bound for, and where we had come from that morning. It was soon realised that two main units were the destination of all of us, either one of the Royal Armoured Corps' regiments or one of the Royal Signals'.

We tried to collect together in groups according to the exact unit, but there would be insufficient room in any compartment for more than just a few. I was surprised to discover that there were quite a number of others who must have travelled in the same train from Kidderminster.

When our train arrived, we discovered it had already brought other recruits from Bristol, or further afield, and there was not very much room in the various carriages. For the first time of many journeys, it would be a case of standing in the corridors for those boarding later. However, I am bound to say that at least in the trains of that era there were corridors for the overflow of passengers rather than the dangerous groupings of extra crowds near the exit doors that are found in modern trains.

Conversation was limited once on board. Everyone seemed to suffer from what I had always believed to be unique, that is, a shutdown brain at times of trauma, thus avoiding reality.

Apart from eating the food provided by our respective homes, and taking the occasional drink from a flask or bottle, much of the journey took place whilst some of us had a series of dreamless sleeps. These were interrupted only by stops at the various stations along the way. The route was to become very familiar over the next two years, and even after all this time I am able to recite the list of calls made en route. Burton on Trent, Tamworth, Derby, Chesterfield, Sheffield, Rotherham, York and Darlington. In recent years there have been some variations to this list north of Sheffield, and of course now, as then, the train continues to Newcastle or beyond.

We picked up more 'reluctant heroes' at each stop, and as predicted the entire train became very crowded, with the ticket collector carrying out his duties in increasingly cramped conditions. At most stops, those boarding far outweighed those leaving. Gradually the food my Mum had carefully packed was being consumed.

Our stop at York was rather longer than those at previous stations, mainly due to the changing of the engine, but that allowed us to see the walls and York Minster, as well as the wonderful construction of the station itself. With me, these things left a lasting impression although the majority of those in the compartment had their minds firmly fixed on other things and probably could not have cared less about the colourful history of York. We were also getting to the end of a long and tiring journey, so could be excused for any failure to be excited by architecture and geography around us.

The railway line between York and Darlington is comparatively straight for a number of miles and in consequence is one of the fastest stretches on the rail system. In the days of steam, especially with a loaded train, there would be much slipping of the driving wheels until eventually the engine gathered sufficient speed and pulled away from the built-up area. Once clear, we accelerated until we were travelling at a speed where the carriages rocked alarmingly. However we were soon to become used to this motion and enjoyed our regular trip over the line. We were, of course, nearing our next point of change, and as we began to see the start of buildings signalling the outskirts of Darlington we started to gather our belongings and rouse ourselves in readiness for another step towards our new life.

As soon as the train came to a halt, doors were opened and the vast majority of the passengers spilled onto the platform, some looking fresh, others dazed, and now looked for the indicator board with the name Richmond. This was not very difficult, and in any case the chaps who had first dismounted were already moving towards a bay platform at which stood a much smaller engine with a few empty coaches. Shuffling slowly, rather like the reluctant schoolboy, we made our way to this new conveyance and squeezed on board until there seemed no room left. However, we waited until another train, this time heading south, pulled into the station and disgorged even more young men who now crossed the bridge and crushed into every spare corner of this new train. I think that we had decided they could not possibly get on board, but somehow they did. Had we been in India, there would have been people sitting on roofs and clinging to the outside of doors, but being Britain, the surplus just stood like upright sardines in a tin.

We soon realised that we were headed back down the line towards York, but after only a few minutes the train turned off the main line and began to pass through meadow and farmland, through small hamlets, and on through unfamiliar scenery into Richmond. This small market town had the somewhat dubious privilege of receiving every fortnight hundreds of new troops on their way to the Catterick Garrison. We later discovered that there was also a station in the centre of Catterick but, owing to limited capacity for engines, it was decided that Richmond was more suited to the mass intake. I felt a fleeting regret for the town having to survive the extra noise and traffic, although the inhabitants somehow seemed to cope with the problems.

My memory of the actual station has faded somewhat, but I can remember there was a large yard with possibly a metal railing round it. Conscription had more or less ended by the time the notorious Dr Beeching closed the line, and with it the station. This closure, carried out under the 'cloak' of economy, was not unique, and indeed many branch lines were erased from the map. Mostly this occurred after an excessive amount of money had been spent on branch lines, thus creating the impression that they were uneconomical. I feel this country has suffered greatly as a result of this series of savage cuts, and it is significant that the private companies which took their place are still serving the public, although it has to be said that not much freight is carried. Stations such as Richmond were closed for ever and now one would not even realise a station had been there.

Once more we clambered out, this time without any real idea of what came next. There were many lorries parked in the yard, each painted with signs and symbols which meant nothing to us, but which showed the regiment from which they had come for us. They would shortly convey us to various destinations, but it was difficult to decipher the various shouts of the NCOs standing by their own vehicle and holding clipboards. It was like a meeting of town criers, each trying to make himself heard over the noise of the others. Many of us stood as if mesmerised, upon which the shouting became louder and more urgent until eventually we became aware which particular screeching we needed to head for. Gradually most became united with the right person, in my case one Lance Corporal Morton, who ticked off our names from his list and almost pushed us over the tailboard of the lorry, on board which were already several of the men who we were soon to get to know and work with.

We sat on the wooden seats on either side of the vehicle, and as soon as the last person was on board Mr Morton climbed into the cab beside the driver and we were off out of the yard as if all the devils in hell were after us. Squashed against our neighbours, and clutching our suitcases containing our few possessions, we lurched in unison with the lorry as it took each corner. Fortunately we could not see out of the back as the heavy tarpaulin had been tied down, and in the darkness we could only guess where we were going. The whine of the four-wheel drive in our ears added to our discomfort and we were quite terrified by this new experience – Army drivers. We were, however, soon to discover that we had less to fear from the maniacs behind the wheel than from our new found mentor Lance Corporal Morton.

After what seemed an eternity, but in all probability was something like fifteen minutes, we rounded the final corner on two wheels (one of them the spare) and screeched to a halt. The tarpaulin was thrown back, the tailgate dropped and, blinking in the sudden daylight, we were 'invited' to get out. The actual phrase was 'Move your arses you 'orrible lot.' We complied with alacrity and found ourselves on a driveway between two green-painted huts, and were ushered into one of them.

Despite our numbed legs, we soon found ourselves passing through an entrance porch, past a washing and toilet area and into a long, narrow room with beds and wooden lockers alternating along both sides. In the centre was a black coke stove sitting in the middle of a concrete square. We were told to choose a bedspace, and I noted there was a rush to get as close to the stove as possible, although it was not yet lit. The reason for wanting to get close to the only heat source was obvious before the first evening was through. Most huts accommodated about twenty-five men in the main area.

Not a single moment was wasted, as was the case for the next few weeks. We had noticed an assortment of mops, brushes, buckets, fire extinguishers, and a large square object on the end of a broom handle, which was called a 'bumper'. With this object, the wooden floors were given a polish, and kept that way.

The bumper was discovered to be an instrument of torture.

'If you want blankets, you had better go to the stores and get kitted out,' we were now told, so leaving our suitcases on our beds as a mark of reservation, we assembled outside and were marched (or should it be shuffled) to the squadron stores.

Chapter Two

A Few Surprises

The badge we were about to wear in our berets (Figure 1) was officially known as the 'Mailed Fist', but to the crude soldiery it was known as the 'Wanking Spanner'.

We reached the stores in double-quick time, and followed the Corporal up the steps into the building where the first thing which greeted us was a large notice. 'God helps those who help themselves, but God help those found helping themselves from these stores'. Nothing could have been clearer, even though we were also told that any items of equipment or uniform we lost would have to

Figure 1   The RAC 'Mailed Fist' badge.

be replaced out of our own pockets. During my service I never became aware of anyone being caught in the act of theft from the stores, although there were cases of misappropriation of stores, unknown to top ranks.

The issue of kit was achieved as swiftly as possible, since the storemen were keen to go off duty and have their tea, though our first experience of Army food made one wonder why. I will try to describe the scene, but anyone who ever saw the film *Carry on Sergeant* will have a pretty good idea of how the issue was carried out. We stood in a long queue which passed slowly along a waist-high wooden counter. Behind this, a line of stores personnel stood with piles of equipment. and just at their rear was a large unit of shelves, equally loaded with many items. As we moved, we were given two pairs of heavy boots, several pairs of drawers cellular (underpants to you), a mug, two plates and a set of eating irons (knife, fork and spoon) fastened together in one unit. Uniform blouses and trousers, berets, webbing equipment, a steel helmet, greatcoat, and denims (overalls) were added, and our bedding, blankets, sheets, pillows and a mattress. The piles in our arms mounted until it became necessary to find somewhere to place the larger objects, whilst we continued collecting. Our final items were clasp knives (complete with gadgets to get boy scouts out of horses' hooves) and a housewife. We were bitterly disappointed to discover that this was merely a small pack containing sewing thread, needles, etc. I am fairly confident in saying that we were not, on this occasion, issued with rifles, since, even without ammunition they might be dangerous in inexperienced hands.

These were issued later so that we had them to commence drilling on the square. Many of the clothing items were issued by guesswork, our various sizes being asked for in the case of berets and battledress.

Many of these were changed for the correct size within the next few days. The berets could be shrunk by putting them into hot water, then immediately into cold, but until we had received our first army haircuts the final size could not be determined accurately.

Most of us required at least three journeys to get all our items back into our barrack room. Fortunately we were allowed to walk back singly rather than together, and soon we each had a pile on the springs of our beds. Most of us knew our shoe sizes, so there was less exchange of boots than of other things. We had needed to sign to say we had received everything, though this was as much guessing as being certain if we had received all we should have. In view of our ignorance on this matter, a few days' tolerance was allowed, though somewhat grudgingly.

Most of us were now hungry, as well as tired, so we were pleased to be shown the location of the mess hall where we would eat our three main meals. There was one exception to this. One person was detailed to remain in the hut to ensure no outsiders came in to thieve our new items. He would eat a little later. The drawer of that particular 'short straw' would have to remain hungry for a little longer. Perhaps he received a better meal as a result of his volunteering, I can only hope so, because the remainder of us suffered with a very unappetizing meal. Some kind of white fish, swimming in a sea of colourless liquid, presumably warm water, was followed by doorsteps of bread with margarine and jam. All this was washed down with char (tea). In this regard, I had a problem which had not been considered until now. I do not drink tea, never have, and I dislike even the smell of it. The overwhelming memory of the first entry to the mess hall is that of the smell. I understand that many lads decided not to tackle the food as a result of the terrible stench of hot and rancid fat. By way of answer to my query as to what I could have to drink, I was shown a cold water tap in our ablutions. Several lads had nasty burns from the scalding liquid out of the tea urns, so I thought myself lucky, but the triumph was short-lived when I discovered that after each meal, we were expected to wash plates, etc. by dipping them into vats of very hot water just outside the building. If you washed everything properly, you risked burning your fingers or, even worse, dropping items into the tank. Those could only be retrieved when the greasy water had been drained.

Owing to our extreme hunger, we ate this rather unpleasant meal, but fortunately either the food was better later, or we became used to it. Mostly the food was greasy, but at least there was more of it.

We walked back to our new home and allowed the chap on guard to go for his tea. There were two pieces of bad news awaiting our return. First, that we would be expected to take part in a country-wide scheme that was taking place throughout the weekend, and which would mean that we would have to take turns at doing guard duty throughout the next three nights. Just as this was sinking in, we were hit with the second piece of bad news. Owing to our recent arrival and the fact that there would be insufficient time to get our uniforms up to standard, when the remainder of the camp went off on Easter leave in ten days' time, we would have to remain behind doing a variety of duties. As a result of the interruption of training during that leave, our basic length of square-bashing would be extended by a fortnight, and we would need to complete eight weeks instead of six. With these happy items of news, Lance Corporal Morton left us to get on with sorting through our equipment and disappeared to have an evening drink in the Corporals' Mess.

Whilst finding places to store our newly acquired kit and making up our beds for the first night, we began to get to know each other. We learned where everyone lived, whether or not they were married or lived with their parents, and what they hoped to achieve during their time in the service. I gathered from the conversation that I was the only sexually inexperienced person in the room, although I learned later that much of the bragging was specially tailored for the rest of us. There was much smoking, quite a bit of cadging of cigarettes, since we were not allowed out to the Naafi just yet, and by now we had the stove lit and were gathered as closely round it as possible to get a share of the warmth. The stove was reluctant to light until we discovered a pile of coal which assisted the ration of coke to catch. The coal belonged to the fellows in the hut next door, and their price for letting us share it was to listen to their stories of how they were doing in the Army. They had been in one whole fortnight. They were anxious to tell us all about the horrors of our training to come, and how expert they were already.

By now, we had a moderately warm hut, but discovered that anyone whose bed was more than a few feet away was literally out in the cold. Items which we could find no room for in our locker were put under the bed, and it was not long before most of us had either got into bed, or were sitting close to the glowing stove. Lights out was at ten thirty, and gradually the conversation died away and most of us fell into a deep sleep.

A fearful noise, swiftly identified as a sadist banging the dustbin lid with a wooden cane, roused us at an unearthly hour the next morning. The banging was accompanied by the demand that we get up, coupled with obscene suggestions as to what we might previously have been doing beneath the blankets. In the famous, well-recorded saying, 'Hands off cocks, on socks.' This was the orderly NCO on his morning rounds. A certain amount of slowness in responding to the shouted instructions evoked more abuse and obscenities, and was no doubt due to our dreaming we were still at home. Having established that we were all on the move, the sadist moved to Mr Morton's room, in the corner of the hut, and gently woke him. Once dressed he was able to continue chasing us into the ablutions. Here, we found that the early birds got most of the hot water for shaving, leaving the rest to do their best with the colder water remaining. There was a limited period in which to complete all essential ablutions, which led in turn to queues for some of the facilities. We were then on our way to breakfast, the only meal which it was compulsory to attend. Failure to eat that meal with a subsequent fainting on parade would lead to being put on a charge, known in the army as a 252. The result of such a charge was appearing in front of the Squadron Leader and probably being punished by having to do 'fatigues'.

I should explain that the RAC, being part of the cavalry, was organised into squadrons as opposed to ordinary platoons as was the case with other army units.

In order to go to breakfast, we were dressed in our new denims, wore berets and boots, gaiters and belts, although for the first few times, we looked more like tramps than soldiers. However, we were allowed to walk to the mess under our own steam, providing we returned in good time for parade.

After the meagre fare of the previous evening, we were somewhat apprehensive and very hungry, so whatever was dished up was eaten ravenously. It was, however, an improvement on the fish.

Pausing only to return our eating equipment – adequately cleaned, we hoped – to our lockers, we were gathered together in one squad and an attempt was made to show us the rudiments of drill and marching. Despite those few extra minutes attempting to show us these vital movements, when we finally moved towards the square it could only be described as a shambles. No amount of swearing or threatening could improve on the limited abilities of most of the group. I had the advantage of previous cadet training but even I was surprised at the very exaggerated movements of proper drill.

Our group was known as serial 5306, which referred to the fact that we were the sixth intake of the year 1953. As the most recent addition to the regiment, we had 'pride of place' at the rear of the square, which also happened to be the highest place, and the most conspicuous.

On this occasion there was little point in our being inspected, although we were swiftly made aware of what would shortly be expected of us when we turned out for parades. We were told that A squadron, in which we now were, was the basic training unit, and if we managed to complete the course and pass out, we would go on to other squadrons for trade training for which we had been selected. We also discovered that above Lance Corporal Morton were Sergeant Martin, and a second lieutenant whose name escapes me. Above them were Captain Stirum and Major Crotty, the latter being responsible for all training. Each of these persons was pointed out to us so that we would recognise them on sight, and Sergeant Martin gave us a list of the things we would be expected to learn.

Meanwhile the remainder of the parade had been dismissed to their various duties, and we stood in isolation listening to a seemingly endless tariff of future events. About this time an attempt was made to teach us to salute properly in case we met an officer on our way round camp. This would only happen if we were in uniform, complete with beret. Most of us grasped the rudiments of the movement, and we now felt we knew what to do when we met someone holding the Queen's commission. Some even started saluting warrant officers, who also tended to wear peaked caps, but this was soon discouraged, and we were taught to look both on shoulders and sleeves in order to identify rank.

We 'marched' away to the squadron office, where the first event was to be issued with our army numbers. These were to be remembered at all times, and would appear on all official documents. I can still recite my number, fifty years on. We then received two pay books. Part One was the booklet we had to carry at ALL times, in or out of uniform, but Part Two was only required on pay day when we went to collect our vast fortunes of twenty-eight shillings per week, with savings of a few shillings being taken off and kept for our demob. Neither part of the pay book was ever to be lost.

It was now time to be interviewed by the PSO (personnel selection officer) who would, with the aid of more tests, decide what our future jobs would be. This was a lengthy process, so a few at a time would wait in the office, whilst the remainder went off to complete some little task or other There were five grades available for which to be selected: potential officer, signaller/gunner, AFV (tank) driver, B4 (lorry) driver or general duty person (cleaners). Each of these would require one form of training or another, the length of the course dependent on the requirements of the job. There was also the strong possibility that, after passing the course, we would be posted overseas to one of the seven regiments which we served. That posting would come after a period in the Drafting Wing, a place with a terrible reputation for hard graft, high standards and severe punishments. Thereafter one would go to the appropriate world location.

Having been at Public School, and having served in two cadet units, I was selected as a potential officer, but this turned out to have mixed blessings. I was regarded by the 'corp' as a useful person to march the squad to places like the mail collection office each day, or to do little jobs, giving him a few extra breaks from the group. However, it also gave him an 'Aunt Sally' on whom to vent some of his spite when he regarded us as useless, which was quite frequent. On these occasions he would blame the shortcomings of all on me, belittling my status by declaring PO (potential officer) 'piss hole'. He obviously regarded me as being better than the others, so this was a back-handed compliment.

Not only would we not be going on 'block' Easter leave, but until we looked like soldiers we would not be allowed out of camp. We could go to the Naafi, wander round between our squadrons or go to official parades or other regiments if part of our training required it, but we were not supposed to proceed outside these parameters. More of that later.

We soon found out that the Naafi could provide us with extra food, to make up for official mess shortcomings, and also drinks, although with the need to keep our minds alert we tended to keep to fruit squashes. During morning breaks cups of tea and a variety of fattening pastries and cakes were available. The canteen also had a shop which sold such necessities as polish, dusters, blanco, Brasso and candles. No, they were not expecting power cuts, but the candles were used beneath the bumper to shine up the wooden floor. Cut into flakes, they were spread over the surface and rubbed into the wood until it shone.

Whilst in the canteen, or if anyone possessed a radio, we could listen to the popular songs of the era, which included one that was rarely off the air. Guy Mitchell singing 'She Wears Red Feathers and a Hula-hula Skirt'. There were rumours that a much larger, better equipped Naafi club existed in the middle of the garrison at the place known as camp centre. It was to be several weeks before we could sample just how good this phantom place really was.

Chapter Three

Troopers' (Privates') Progress

Our initiation into guard duty, this first weekend, was traumatic. It was cold, misty and dark, and we were allotted two-hour tours of duty during which we were expected to roam round the immediately placed huts (probably about half a dozen). With four-hour rests following our two-hour duties, there was just sufficient time to get warm again and have a short sleep before being roused once more to resume patrol. I remember one of my tours was between 1.00 a.m. and 3.00 a.m. – probably the worst time to be doing such a rotten job. We were warned that it was a serious offence to go to sleep whilst on guard, but most of us tried to find some shelter or the least cold patch in order to lean against one of the barracks, or even a convenient bush or tree. With pauses for food, ablutions and other essential matters, this scheme continued to occupy us either on guard, or in other duties, for the next three days. In between, we were allowed to make a start on getting our new equipment and uniforms into some kind of order, polishing, pressing and generally getting to grips with the numerous articles.

Outsize berets had to be shrunk, as already mentioned. Brass objects and small items required smoothing and polishing. We discovered that pieces of box cardboard with Brasso on made good smoothers. All webbing had to be scrubbed white before being covered with several layers of blanco, neither too thick nor too thin, and this had to be carefully avoided when polishing attached brasses. However, the real nightmare was the boots. When given to us, their entire surface was pitted and, in order to achieve a satisfactory shine, the leather needed to be smoothed. This was achieved by heating the handle of one's spoon on the red-hot stove, and gently burning the pits away. Too much heat and the leather burned, meaning at best more hard work, and at worst a new pair of boots. Experience showed the most effective method was several gentle applications of the spoon, carefully checking the result after each scorching. Once there was a smooth surface on which to work, the real hard work began. Layers of polish, mixed with one's own spit, were gently applied to create a surface shine. Most of us mixed the two ingredients in the open polish tin, but it sounds much easier than it was. Many of us took several weeks of hard graft to obtain the desired result on both pairs of boots, plenty of Kiwi or Cherry Blossom being used in the process. It was also known that if the boots were not to standard on inspection, their being thrown accross the room did little to assist the shine being built-up.

An item known as a button stick was used to support and isolate greatcoat buttons and cap badges from surrounding material whilst in the course of polishing. Finally, we had to learn how to put the pieces of webbing equipment together properly, and how to display all items for inspections. There was a correct way to do this, illustrated on a photograph which was passed round the room until we managed to get the display correct.

We had all items of equipment and uniform to prepare, although it would be some time before they reached the required standard. Meanwhile our civilian clothes had to be packed in brown paper parcels and posted home. This included ordinary shoes, so we never wore shoes for eight weeks. We were warned to change our socks daily, because the large amount of marching we would be doing created heat, and possibly blisters. Most of us got plenty of those, however careful we were in changing our socks.

Although we had been at Catterick for four or five days, no one at home had even heard if we had arrived safely. They were expected to rely on the old maxim, that bad news travels fast, presumably. Now, however, we were allowed to write to give our new address, and say we were there. Perhaps thereafter we could then expect some post. Looking at my address I now realise it was a good job there were no postal codes in those days, otherwise most envelopes would have been too small to get it all on. Mine read as follows:

22861872 Trooper Kettle M
Serial 5306
A Squadron
Menin Lines
65th Training Regiment
Royal Armoured Corps
Catterick Camp
Yorks

In addition to personal equipment, it was expected that all features of our hut, from floor to loos, would be kept in perfect condition, clean, bright and shining, the stove painted black, concrete areas white, and all surfaces wiped down. Razor blades were used to scrape all wooden handles of brooms, etc., and that instrument of torture, the 'bumper', was used over the floor. Once the floor had been shone, no one dared walk over it. Every Wednesday the Squadron Leader, Major Cruikshank, would inspect all barracks in his area, accompanied by the Squadron Sergeant Major and relevant NCOs. On the first occasion, a measure of tolerance was shown, owing to our recent arrival, but afterwards there would be no excuse for any shortcomings. The results of substandard inspections was rather like a less pleasant version of being married to a schoolteacher; she makes you keep doing it until you get it right! Individual failure to meet the standard resulted in unpleasant jobs in the cookhouse and elsewhere, doing fatigues for one or more nights according to the severity of the crime. That also put one further back in reaching the standard.

At every opportunity we were practising marching and foot drill, in the hope that on our first serious parade we might at least be able to keep in step and come to attention properly. It turned out to be a forlorn hope since several members of the squad did not know their left from their right, and there is always one 'Corporal Jones' whose movements are always half a beat behind the remainder. I certainly recognised these symptoms whilst watching *Dad's Army* in later years, and know the writers must have studied trainee squads to obtain the character. I am pleased to say the one behind the rest was never me.

We were starting to get used to each other, learning which chaps could be relied on, and which not. Under Queen's Regulations we were forbidden to discuss religion or politics, so inevitably the topic of conversation ended up as sex. On such occasions, this reluctant virgin kept pretty quiet. However, as already implied, I now believe many of the claims could be regarded as products of the imagination, or wishful thinking. Undoubtedly some of the stories were true, which kept us amused and interested, to say nothing of envious.

In the first week or so, regular visits were made to the MI (Medical) room for a series of jabs to counter a variety of possible conditions including tetanus and tuberculosis. We would stand in a very long line, sleeves rolled up, waiting for the orderly to proceed along with the syringe. Those at the rear would experience the discomfort of blunt needles. Many of us experienced unpleasant side-effects from the various vaccines pumped into our arms, including high fever and soreness, but since the routine for reporting sick was so complicated most of us preferred to suffer in silence. The Corporal, in his usual manner, insisted that the best cure was to circulate the blood by getting on to the square and marching until exhausted, swinging the arms even more than usual. No one who had unpleasant symptoms received any sympathy and there were few who escaped altogether from nasty feelings.

About the same time I suffered badly with a continuous series of sore throats, rather like bad tonsilitis. I eventually decided that it was due to the water I was drinking from the cold taps. It was also at such visits to the MI room that further FFIs (free from infection) checks were made on our private parts, causing more embarrassment.

The army certainly had plenty of effective ways to keep our noses to the grindstone, mostly under the threat of punishment. As a result of a moderate misdemeanour, we could be put on a charge resulting in an official hearing in front of the squadron leader. More serious matters would then go before the commanding officer. In extreme cases, and after a very serious breach of conduct, there were courts martials, but these were rare among newer recruits. Any minor wrongdoing could be dealt with by your own NCOs without going on your record, usually resulting in extra drill, being confined to one's hut, or by fatigues. To go on fatigues meant that for one or more nights you did menial tasks, followed by an appearance on the late-night parade with guards and other duties, this held at 10.00 p.m. in the drill shed. This was rather like a large barn and was at least covered in inclement weather.

Another punishment was to be put on Fire Picket, although I cannot recall what that involved.

I have already mentioned that the most likely place to be sent on fatigues was the cookhouse. It often involved cleaning greasy pieces of equipment, but was more likely to include peeling spuds. On one occasion, I told the cook corporal that I had heard the army had machines for peeling the mounds of potatoes; he replied that it was true, and that I was the latest model. That was the last time I stuck my neck out on such a matter. As you can see, I was put on this punishment several times. One evening I was given a stack of corned (bully) beef tins to open. I had been warned to look out for the sharp edges, but somehow managed to gash my thumb rather badly. It bled profusely for several hours, and I was more careful afterwards. For me, the hardest part of the punishment was that late parade. Even though you were dressed for hard work, you were still expected to appear neat and tidy. You were usually tired, and the waiting around was irksome. It did not help that you usually had tired and irritable orderly officers and NCOs taking the parade.

Several times during our busy weekly schedule we would be marched to the gymnasium for a session of PT. This stood for physical training, although for me it was more a case of physical torture. We were kept very busy by the ultra-fit instructors, climbing ropes, vaulting, sprinting, exercises and the like, but the most demanding part was the speed at which we were expected to undress and dress before and after the sessions. A time limit was imposed to complete the clothing exchange, with the promise that the last three to get ready would have to double round the square. In fact I never remember anyone doing this, but it had the desired effect. Mind you, the experience has proved useful during some amorous adventures since then!

In a small caravan, at the crossroads between A and C squadrons, was a man we all called the 'Spiv'. He was surrounded by a large collection of items for sale, regimental badges, lanyards, embroidered silk handkerchieves and the like, either for us to use or to buy for relatives or friends. I bought a hankie with the regimental badge on for Mum, which she kept for the rest of her life. Some of the more ornate items were not approved as official, and so most things became mementos. Certainly the Spiv seemed to make a good living out of the trade from passing soldiery.

By the middle of our second week, we had all received our gradings from the PSO and now had some inkling of what to expect from the months ahead. However, we had to get down to some really hard work in basic training, including fieldcraft, map reading, handling weapons (including taking them to pieces and restoring them), firing on the ranges, learning Queen's Regulations, and marching and even more marching. Some lessons were taken by L/C Morton, others by regular soldiers with experience in particular subjects. In between we attended training films, and, for a little light relief we were shown pictures of male genitals which had been exposed to various types of venereal disease. This had a sobering effect on the sexual appetite for a while, but after the initial shock, most still could not wait to 'get their leg over'. I suppose it was rather like going to the theatre, a good performance could lead to the clap!

We were starting to get the hang of army life. This did not mean we liked it, but it was by now a familiar routine. We knew what was expected of us even if we were still a long way from attaining the high standard demanded. Perhaps the biggest change in our appearances was the hair-cut, which changed even the 'Teddy Boy' fashion into a very short back and sides.

We were very aware that shortly many of the 30,000 strong Catterick garrison would be going home for Easter. Like so many things in life, the full implications had still not penetrated our brains, but on Good Friday morning we were unable to ignore what was going on around us. A large fleet of buses arrived on the square, and were directed into position. They were labelled for various destinations and, after being filled to capacity, each left to meet the appropriate train leaving from Darlington station. Richmond was not used because it was too small to cope with such large numbers on a tight schedule. As one would expect, the departure and timing of every bus and train was exact to dovetail, and there would be some eight or nine trains leaving during the day.

Those of us left behind could only envy the others, and, despite my confidence that I would not suffer from home-sickness, the beginnings of that malady were already starting to show. We had been given different tasks to perform around the camp during the coming week, which would keep us busy and help keep the camp 'ticking over'. My job was to clean and look after the Officers' Club, so I needed to leave our own lines to get there.

Chapter Four

Trying to Become Soldiers

I suppose the fact that I had to leave the, by now, familiar area of our squadron, in order to do my duties at the Officers Club increased the chance of this homesickness. The fact was that leaving our lines and moving around brought me more into contact with the general public, and with buildings and things which reminded me of normal life and home. The shock of this change was somewhat akin to leaving the womb, and I was unprepared for the results, despite having already been away at school.

The type of effect of such a different life could only be described as a culture shock.

The weather was quite cold with snow flurries over the early part of the week. Comparative silence reigned over the camp as we commenced our various jobs. My duties were varied, and included such tasks as rolling the tennis courts, cleaning out grates, polishing furniture, and general tidying. We were given lunch each day, after the residents had eaten, our choice being similar to the main club menu. This led to my learning another important lesson in life. Never assume that a name means the same as something with which you are vaguely familiar. My choice that first day was curried egg, and I jumped at the chance to sample some newish dish. Of course in those days, the general public was not so familiar with spicy dishes, since Indian and other Oriental eating places were still unknown.

I took one mouthful and realised that this was really hot. So much so that I needed several glasses of water to restore my mouth to normal temperature. No doubt the cooks had been trained overseas, possibly in India, and they certainly made their curries very hot. Fortunately there were other items available, and so I was able to have lunch of a more familiar kind. It was several years before I tried curry again, and I now like them fairly hot, but they never attain the same heat as that one in Catterick.

The work was not particularly demanding, leading to plenty of spare time and breathing space, which in turn led to improvements in the standard of our equipment. Possibly being left behind was a blessing in disguise although we did not see it as such at the time. Certainly we were never idle, although we had more time to think than normal. Probably the worst aspect was the extension of our training period from six to eight weeks.

I was shocked by the severity of the homesickness, and if ever there was a time when I was tempted to abscond, that was it, but the consequences would have been too severe.

The week eventually passed, most of the garrison strength had returned to duty, except one or two who had decided they preferred it at home. They soon found the Military Police knocking on their door, telling them how much they were being missed. Even with the excuse of a domestic crisis to settle, the result was just not worthwhile. Being absent without official leave (AWOL) was considered a serious crime, even with mitigating circumstances, when a measure of leniency was shown. Anyone thinking that by failing to return, they would shorten their length of service, was due for disappointment, as the time would normally be added on at the end, and could include time spent in military prison, which, by all accounts was not very pleasant.

We were now really back in training with a vengeance. There was to be no let-up for the remainder of the initial period either in standard of accommodation, personal equipment, or achievement. Anyone who believes the storyline in the film *Carry on Sergeant*, already quoted, that a bunch of hopeless misfits could pick up enough ability and smartness in twenty-four hours to win their way to champion platoon is unaware of the reality. To become top in everything required total effort for the entire length of training. If you failed to attain the standard quite early on in the work, then you were 'backsquadded', that is, you joined the next lower intake and had to go through everything again from the start. The character in the film who was continually sent back until at last he passed out on his final day of service, in fact could not have achieved this, but it made an interesting human story. Our ability to march and to drill, either with or without rifles, gradually improved, and in ability and appearance, we began to look more like soldiers than ragamuffins.

All this time, the Korean war was raging. As an added threat to make us behave, we were made aware that Korea, with all its horrors, was where miscreant soldiers were sent. The thought of such a cold and dangerous battleground very swiftly had us toeing the line.

We had been introduced to the army barber by a quick march to the barber's shop. Sweeney Todd had nothing on them – they were up-and-over merchants with no regard for style, shape, or feelings. I frequently look at modern fashions and wonder if those sporting the 'bald' look would be so keen if it became compulsory. After completion of our 'Maison Catterick' cuts, we were not so far short of that style, and berets which had previously fitted were now a shade too large.

Mind you, there was no point in reducing the size even further since the hair soon grew back. One lad I met later in my service, had no problems with the barber – he had no hair whatsoever growing on his body or on his head.

We had discovered that, in addition to the Naafi, there was a very good fish 'n' chip shop just over the road. Technically, we were breaking the rules to walk across there and collect the succulent Yorkshire goodies, but since we went over in denims, and the guardroom was out of sight in the other direction, we managed to get away with this regular trip. It made a change from the Naafi fare of eggs, beans and chips, although both meals were pleasant compared with food provided in the mess hall. I am only surprised that it has taken so long for quality chip shops like Harry Ramsden's to become established elsewhere.

Making progress? We thought so, although our instructors had other opinions. There were occasions when kit had to be laid out two or three times in order to obtain a grudging acceptance that it was up to standard. We were desperate to be able to wear our uniforms in public, and both sets of battledress were good enough for that, although the best uniform, worn on parades and special occasions, needed to be just that little bit better. Hours of 'bumping' put a real shine on the floor, only to be ruined by someone who spilt Brasso over it, thus making us start again. There was a constant battle between having the stove alight to keep warm, or leaving it unlit and clean. Beds were lined up with string to ensure perfectly straight lines.

The end of our training was approaching. We had succeeded in gaining satisfactory marks in shooting, and in the theoretical subjects in the classroom, and at least we were marching as one person and not like a group of out-of-step tramps.

Passing-out parade was scheduled for a Thursday, exactly eight weeks after we first arrived. Parents and friends were invited to attend, but for most it was either too far to travel, or they were at work. In any case, we would have had very little time to devote to them, since our last hours were spent in perfecting everything.

The previous night, resplendent in our second-best outfits, we were let loose on the town. Just imagine freedom after so long! Some went to the Naafi club in camp centre, whilst others, including myself, opted for a quiet country pub on the back road to Richmond. There was a risk that after so long without drink, hair would be let down (those who had any left), but since our return would be past the guardroom, where an inspection was likely, most of us remained reasonably sober. However, when we left the pub after a couple of pints of cider and got into the considerably cooler atmosphere outside, there was a certain amount of giggling and frolicking. We reached our hut without getting into trouble, and sat polishing everything ready for the next morning.

The big day dawned bright and clear; it was a perfect day for impressing the inspecting officers, then for going home on seventy-two hours' leave. Under the watchful eyes of Lance Corporal

Morton, Sergeant Martin, and our troop officer, we had one or two final practices along the edge of the square until it was time to march into position in the centre. There was no band to beat out the step, and we relied on silent counting to ensure we were all together. Fortunately there were no 'Corporal Joneses' on the big day to let the side down. Only a handful of visitors were present, but all our regiment's top brass and representatives from northern command attended. Not only was it known as a 'passing-out parade' but due to the fact that the NCO in charge of the best squad was presented with a 'silver stick', that was an alternative title. We did not win that honour, but neither did we disgrace ourselves.

Once the parade was over, and we had been fed in the mess, we were anxious to get on our way to catch a suitable train from Darlington. Fate, however, had other ideas. Pay parade in those days was at 4.00 p.m. on Thursdays, and we would not be allowed to go until we had attended this. It did not take long to work out that, by waiting until 4.30, we were likely to miss all the connections we had planned. We all wanted to get out of camp so we went to Darlington where we could find the times of the next train. In my case, it would not be until around 8.00 p.m., so I telephoned home to tell them. This meant that Mum and Dad would have to drive to Birmingham, since the last bus would have gone by the time we arrived in New Street.

In the time we had to spare after the parade, we packed everything we were not wearing and took it over to our new squadrons, in my case C, and deposited them in the stores, bedding and all. As a potential officer, I was to enter the Dismounted Wing, after leave. This title was left over from the old cavalry days when those off normal duties would leave their horses behind, and become dismounted.

At Darlington, we found food in the buffet and just sat around until our various trains were due. The benches were hard, but later in my service I was to discover that the table in that waiting room is even harder.

You may remember that all our civilian clothes, including shoes, had been posted home. Consequently we had to travel in boots, and

A typical group of trainees. Photograph courtesy of Mr J. Smith.

because we had sent the second-best boots into the stores, we were left travelling in our best boots. It had taken weeks to reach their high gloss, to say nothing of much swearing and sweating, so on a packed train I found myself moving them out of the way whenever anyone came near me. Needless to say, I could not avoid some contact, resulting in some damage and my working on them all over the weekend to get them up to standard again. Fortunately we were able to travel back to camp in our shoes with the boots carefully wrapped out of harm's way.

There was so much to tell my parents about, and with them having family news for me, we were very late going to bed. For my part, I could have enjoyed a lie-in next morning, but I wanted to go to town to meet friends and show off my uniform. However, I had forgotten it was Friday, and most of them were at work. I met some people I knew in town and they seemed impressed with my appearance, but most of the reunions would have to wait for Saturday, especially the evening dance where I could impress a few girls.

My leave was due to end at 2359 hours on the Sunday evening, and it seemed no time at all before we were discussing the train times for the return journey. It would not be advisable to risk being late back, so it was necessary to catch a mid-afternoon train from New Street. I had been too tired to want to drive the car on the way home, but now I was happy to take the wheel direct to Birmingham, since there was no suitable connection from Kidderminster. Very soon I was back on a station platform saying goodbye. Clutching some food in one hand and my best boots in the other, I made certain that they remained untouched. Just as well: my premonition that there would be an early inspection proved all too true.

The journey like so many to come, was busy and tiring. There were always other service people travelling home, or back to camp, and in those days our railways were efficient and comparatively cheap.

Chapter Five

To Be (or not to be) an Officer

On arrival in camp, I woke the duty storeman to request my bedding and kit bag, full of (by now) creased clothing. One of the first tasks next day would be to iron this into acceptable shapes and sizes, but first a night's sleep – well, part of a night. Other arrivals were constantly disturbing those of us in our beds, banging their gear into their lockers and creaking the various bedsprings, just like a hotel honeymoon suite. We were finally brought back from whatever catnaps we had achieved, by the orderly NCO doing his imitation of Buddy Rich on the dustbin lid. When he was satisfied that no one could possibly have remained unaware that it was time to get up, he left our hut to go and upset the others. We achieved our various ablutions and went to breakfast in a new mess hall. The only difference between A and C squadrons' eating arrangements was the location of the building, since the same greasy pile of what passed for food ended up on our carefully held plates. I say carefully since it was not unknown for someone's attention to be distracted, and to suddenly discover that every item on offer had been put on the same plate. This resulted in a mixture of porridge and kippers needing to be separated, or eaten together, as the mood dictated.

We were about to discover that A squadron had been a picnic, and that what we had considered to be hard work paled into insignificance when placed beside the Dismounted Wing. Instead of having one lance corporal chasing our tails from morning until night, we now had two hard-nosed sergeants whose main aim in life was to reduce everyone to a quivering jelly. Our gear, ourselves and our billet had to be 'shit hot' and nothing less would do. Messrs Bingham and Bowers, for those were the names they were born with (yes, despite our thoughts to the contrary, they had been born), were hell personified, and inspected every single item, both army-supplied and personal, at least once per day. More, if the first inspection revealed any faults. Woe betide anyone with a fleck of soap on the razor, and anything not being worn at the time was to be squared off with cardboard. It had to be exactly to regulation size and placed in the exact position demanded. Spare boots required polishing underneath as well as on top, and spare bootlaces were to be coiled in a ring, tied in place, and polished with black boot polish. There being little time for extra kit layouts, the punishment for offenders was doubling round the square in full webbing, carrying a rifle above the head. A singularly uncomfortable event.

One thing missing from the old A squadron punishment list was fatigues. There was no time for them in the Dismounted Wing, and there was sufficient other punishment for them not to be needed.

Morning parades revealed that our new 'guardian angels' had a sense of humour, despite all appearances to the contrary, twisted though it might have been. It was a crude sense of humour too, but probably the only one they were likely to reveal. This morning 'joke' concerned a lad named Bradbury who, it was revealed, had formed a liaison with one of the Naafi girls, whose name was Mona. Each time we gathered together for morning parade, he was treated to the same question 'Did you cock Mona last night, Bradbury?' and the two would end up in fits of laughter. It is to his credit that he never once answered the question, so no one ever knew.

Our daytime training now consisted of preparation for the War Office Selection Board (WOSB) which we would need to undergo if we wished to obtain the Queen's Commission. The idea was to test our qualities of leadership, though I never discovered a proper qualification in either sergeant to determine which of us were gifted in that direction. We carried out assault courses and endless command tasks, which involved taking groups of men through imaginary obstacles, using a minimum of specified equipment. I found most of it to be inadequate, but then a bad workman always blames his tools. Each of us would take turns to lead the group and to make all the decisions concerning how the task should be achieved. I was already having serious doubts over my ability to get through this schedule. We had to take our squad in more drill, but at least I was comfortable with this aspect, after experience in the cadets. Our masters were seldom satisfied at the results.

No one knew when it would be our turn to go to WOSB, so we were kept hard at these tasks in case the appointment was sooner rather than later. About three weeks into the course we were taken on to the moors for a day and night exercise. Armed with .22 rifles with which to shoot stray pheasants on the way, Messrs Bingham and Bowers took us in lorries to various locations on the loneliest section of that area.

They dropped us off in pairs with no map, and only a compass bearing to follow for a given distance. We had no idea where we would end up or how long it was likely to take. We had full packs and equipment, rifles and a supply of blank ammunition, the total weight of which was heavy enough on a warm spring day. We were told that when we arrived at the destination there would be food and drink, and, hopefully, the rest of our group.

I cannot remember the name of the man who was paired with me for this part of the exercise. All I can remember is that the moor can be an unforgiving, not to say even a dangerous place, with bogs, hillocks, and hidden holes to negotiate, and even large pools of water to walk round. We seemed to be on the move for hours, and there were several times when I, at least, gave up hope of finding our destination safely in the forseeable future. We had been required to leave any money in camp, although there were no shops or market traders from whom to buy food or, even more important, drink. Certainly it appeared to be a matter of survival.

As in all the best novels, just when all our hopes were beginning to fade, we saw the flash of a piece of bright metal shining in the distance. At about the same time, the roof of a building came into view as we descended into yet another valley. At least we had reached civilisation. The building turned out to be the pub where we should rendezvous, and the flash was the sun shining on the rank badge worn by sergeants in some cavalry regiments over the stripes on their right arms. We had arrived. We were fully expecting that we would be the last to arrive, and were surprised to learn that only about half the squad had made it so far. We were given food and drink and allowed to relax on the grass outside the pub to wait for the remainder of the group. The food was bully-beef sandwiches and the drink a refreshing pint of cider, but no one was fussy and we ate all we were given. Over the next hour the rest of the group arrived, and no one was missing. The late-comers had less time to relax before we began the next phase of the exercise.

We were now assembled and told where we must go from the pub. We still had no maps, but were told in some detail the general direction. The plan was that, after dark, the sergeants and the lorry drivers would form an enemy force and locate themselves somewhere along our line of movement. We would need to use fieldcraft techniques to attack them. One of us would be elected leader and would make the decisions and give the orders. At least, that was the theory, but it did not turn out as had been planned.

Reluctantly leaving that little oasis of calm behind us, we set out along dusty country lanes in the expectation that we might use our blank ammunition against those two bullies. We had blackened our faces and tried to appear like proper commandos. We passed one or two cottages and isolated farms, but later found a village where a dance was in progress. Our passing caused quite a stir in the dance hall – I think the youngsters thought the Russians had landed. However, we explained who we were and left them in peace.

By now, it was pitch black and we had no light between us, not even a match; surprise, surprise, we were lost and every lane going away from the one we were on brought forth arguments as to which way we should go. The thirst that had been quenched by the cider was now returning, but there was not even a water bottle to sip at. Mother Fortune smiled on us at that point. At the top of a farm track was a wooden stand, and on this was a milk churn. Having established that it was full, we devised a cunning plan. The combined strength of several lads enabled the churn to be lifted, and with the lid placed on the stand milk was poured into it. From there we could use our mugs to obtain drinks. After replacing the lid and churn we went on our merry way, but I often wondered what the collection agency said to the farmer when they discovered less milk than they should have had.

We had, of course, slowed down considerably through a combination of tiredness and uncertainty about which way to go, and by now the earlier enthusiasm at the prospect of a battle had waned. We had still seen nothing of the 'enemy'. It would have been around midnight when we became aware of flares, thunderflashes, and other noise not far ahead. It could only be our welcoming party. Not only had the sergeants given up on us, but they were now actually searching for us. They too had lost the enthusiasm for a fight. They bollocked us for our total uselessness, and led us to some warm cocoa. They were camped in a large field, and not surprisingly were narked that they had been unable to ambush us and show their skills off. Our beds for the night were our groundsheets, with packs for pillows, but although not comfortable we were very soon asleep.

At sunrise we were woken, shown a cold stream in which to wash and shave, then given a good breakfast of tinned bacon, bread and marmalade, and hot tea. I filled my mug with water from the stream, but made certain that it was upstream from where everyone had washed. There had been quite a heavy dew overnight and some of our equipment was damp, but we had little time to bother about that fact. We piled into the lorries, and relaxed. Here we were on the way back to camp. About three miles from our barracks, the vehicles stopped, and we were made to get out. We had reckoned without either the wrath or the vindictiveness of our masters. I never discovered if it was a punishment for our failure of the previous night, or had been pre-planned as part of the test, but whatever way, it came as a nasty shock.

We marched back in good order, and on reaching the hut, gratefully sat down to take off our equipment, but it was still not over. 'Out on the square,' they yelled, and we then had an hour of serious drill.

During the various horrors of our training schedule and before we had been long in the wing, three things of note happened which remain in my memory. It was the time of the coronation of Her Majesty the Queen. A celebratory ball was held in Hooge Gymnasium for officers and senior non-commissioned ranks, and some of us were volunteered to act as stewards and waiters at the event At very short notice, black trousers, white shirts and accessories were produced, and made to fit. We were given instructions on the taking of orders and serving them to guests; most of the drinks were to be paid for, and we had to take the cash and give out the change. Food, which was free, was also to be served as required.

As the evening wore on, we discovered that many had drunk quite an amount of alcohol, and were not too certain if they were getting the right change. With some cash from that situation, and some from tips, we ended up with a profitable evening.

The second memorable event was Coronation Day itself. We were given a day's holiday, and were free to spend it in camp or elsewhere. One friend who had a motorbike and who lived comparatively close in Scarborough offered to take me to his home to watch the ceremony on TV. I accepted the invitation, and we set out in good time. A chance to get away from the environment of the Dismounted Wing could not be overlooked.

Those who were around at the time will remember that June 2nd 1953 turned out to be a cold, wet, miserable day. On the pillion of a small motorbike, it was very unpleasant indeed. Before we had gone ten miles our greatcoats were saturated, and being unused to riding pillion I was most unhappy at the way in which I was supposed to lean over with the driver, and nearly caused a few upsets. Add to that the bumping of that bike on every uneven patch of road and it was a recipe for a miserable outing. When we arrived, we found that all the friends and neighbours of his parents were crowded into the small lounge, and we found seats right at the back. Little wonder that I cannot remember much of the day's events.

Our return journey was not much more pleasant, and I was not surprised not to be invited on the back of his motorbike thereafter.

The third event concerned cricket. The regiment had a team, and since I had failed dismally to make any of the school teams, I had hopes of getting involved now. One of my grandfathers had been quite an expert, although I had not inherited his talent. However, the standard of regimental cricket was quite high, and once more I was disappointed. They did, however, appreciate my knowledge of the game, and invited me to score on occasion. On one of those occasions I accompanied the team on a short tour of the North West of England, during which a match was played against the boys of St Bees public school, not far from Whitehaven.

The regiment had its own coach. No, not the sort that teaches the game, the kind that takes you from place to place! We travelled in this rather ramshackle conveyance which, with much persuasion and a certain amount of skill from the driver, a trooper called Raven, reached the school in time for the scheduled pitching of wickets. I cannot recall who won, or even if only one day was needed, but another match, or at least the end of that one, took place the next day. It was therefore during the next afternoon that we started back for Catterick. We stopped in Penrith, and were allowed to wander round and find a meal. I settled for the George Hotel, where I found fresh salmon on the menu. Philistine that I was, I assumed this would taste like the tinned variety with which I was familiar, and was disappointed at the taste and shocked by the final bill. Another sharp curve in my learning process.

As instructed, we gathered at the bus, and already realised that our return to camp would be quite late. It was then that Capt Stirum (he of the training section) appeared and stated that as he had his car nearby, he could offer a lift to a couple of us, cutting the return time considerably. Guess who stuck his hand up?

After reaching the main road, it became obvious where Capt Stirum had spent his spare time – in one or more of the local bars. His driving was not too erratic, but he was in a hurry to get back and put his foot down. We were making good progress over the moors, and I was thinking of those 'poor sods' who were stuck in the coach, when he decided to overtake another vehicle without being able to see very far ahead. Half way past, another vehicle was heading straight for us, only it was a lorry and larger than we were. Somehow he managed to brake and pull back behind the car he had started to overtake. Our respective guardian angels must have been with us that night, there was not even a scratch on either vehicle. How a collision was avoided I cannot say, but it was very close indeed. To this day, I will never accept a lift from anyone whose driving I do not know and respect, and certainly not with anyone who has been drinking. I still shudder to think what could have happened.

It appears that WOSB was still not ready for me, and I am certain I was not ready for it. The appointment was still several weeks away, so in order to keep us occupied, some of us were sent on a six week wireless operators course, in a different part of the squadron. We would have to complete one of these sometime in our service anyway, so why not now? We went with great delight, because although we still had Bingham and Bowers breathing down our necks during inspections, at least we could escape them during the day. Our new instructor was another sergeant, one Len Pailing, a ruddy-faced rotund man with the task of teaching us all about wireless and the equipment it used. He had a moustache and was far less regimental than our other three-stripers. Also, he had a crude sense of humour but his fun and casual way was far more relaxed, and we learned quickly from him. Most of what he taught us could seemingly be equated with sex, or with females, but as I say he succeeded in holding our attention and got the best out of the group. For information to penetrate many brains, it is useful to have a good reason to remember, such as having little phrases by which to recall the order of things. One example of his successful teaching concerns a situation where one ground station was out of touch with another, and the message to be sent had to be relayed via a third party. The correct wording for that third party to accept responsibility to relay the message was 'through me, over', which Len likened to a willing girlfriend allowing one to have intercourse with her.

It was Len who first showed me the reason for army instructors being more successful at getting the message across than most civilian teachers. He made the course interesting, treated us as having brains, even though we often seemed to fail to grasp the simplest things, and was the first NCO to make us feel human. Of course, to train soldiers to march and drill requires more bullying than persuasion, so it is a case of horses for courses.

We travelled round the countryside practising our knowledge, and the six weeks passed like a flash.

Having passed the course, we were now ready to face the next stage in trying to become officers.

In the Dismounted Wing were a number of other public school lads. Not, like me, from minor schools, but from the big names like Marlborough, Stow, Uppingham, or even Harrow and Eton, although I think most from these last two were more likely to go to Sandhurst and then into the Brigade of Guards. However, not only were they from famous schools, but there were also famous family names. The two I can remember best were Talbot-Ponsonby, whose family was involved in show-jumping at Olympia, amongst other things, and Fenwick whose claim to fame was the well-known high-class department store in London, Newcastle and elsewhere. Peter Fenwick became a good friend and we ended up going onto the course together.

The WOSB examination was a three and a half day event, which took place in Barton Stacy near Andover in Hampshire. The planning time was designed to complete two full courses per week. One was Sunday to mid-Wednesday, the other mid-Wednesday to Saturday. Peter and I were booked to attend the one which commenced on Sunday, so we were issued with rail warrants to travel viaLondon, and allowed to leave Catterick early on the Saturday morning, thus giving us almost a day in the capital. Once more, it was necessary to travel from Darlington, this time to King's Cross. The journey to Darlington was by now becoming a familiar run from the camp. As I have indicated, although we were from very different backgrounds, there was a rapport between Peter and me and we were quite close friends by now. Our respective overnight accommodation in the metropolis, however, was to be very different, but prior to that, we had a few visits to make. First, we called on the family store in Bond Street, then paid a visit to Peter's brother's flat, and after lunch we went to the Crystal Palace to watch motorcycle racing. The latter was a new experience for me, and I suspect for Peter also. The thrill of actually being there was far greater than watching in the cinema, for television was still in its early days so sport was not very prominent. Solo machines produced average thrills, but it was the sidecar events that had us gasping at the intrepid riders and even more daring passengers. Since that day, I have never received as much excitement from any sporting event, with the exception of my first experience of live steeplechase horse racing.

Peter went to spend the night in his brother's comfortable luxury flat in Berkeley Square, whilst I spent a rather restless night on a solid unit laughingly called a bed, at the Union Jack club, a Services' type of cheap hotel, at the cost of one shilling and sixpence per night, plus extra for breakfast. I have to be fair; I believe that Peter would have invited me to Berkeley Square had there been a room available, but I most likely would not have slept well in any strange bed.

We met up at Waterloo station the next morning, most probably at one of the newspaper stands. We had been told that included in our testing would be questions on current affairs, on world events and other vital topics. Between us, we purchased half a dozen of the most intellectual Sunday papers which, even in those days were quite bulky. It was, of course, impossible to even scratch the surface of the content of these publications on such a comparatively short journey, and I realised how little notice I had been taking of news in recent months, and sadly I learned too little, too late.

We were collected from the station by the usual four-wheel drive truck, which I seem to remember was driven a little less dangerously than by members of wheels troop in Catterick. We were shown to superior accommodation, and told that, for the period of our stay, we would be treated like officers. Tablecloths on tables, waiters serving and the like. On top of our uniforms, we wore coloured rugby shirts to denote which of the four groups we were in. These were to make for easy identification. There were to be no duties, only a daily routine, after which we would be free to go into nearby towns. However, with all this unfamiliar freedom and treatment, we would be under constant surveillance, and expected to act and behave like gentlemen. This was to continue throughout the length of the course. There were various interviews, including the one we already anticipated, asking about current and foreign affairs. I was just as unprepared for that one as for the others, so all the newspaper purchases had been a waste of cash.

The largest part of our time was taken in the assessment of our leadership qualities, by continually performing those awful command tasks which I hated so much. There never seemed enough of the right kind of equipment, and I was really floundering. Every member of the squad took it in turns to take control, and we were given different tasks each time, so no one could copy another candidate. It took me less than a day and a half to realise that I had little hope of passing this demanding test, I was just not mature enough. At the end of the course, we were immediately notified if we had passed or failed. It came as no surprise to find myself in the latter group. Those who passed would get seven days' leave, then be posted to Mons Barracks, Aldershot, or some similar officer cadet school where further success would grant them a commission as a second lieutenant. Peter passed, and I never met him again.

Officers would be required to purchase their own uniforms, and pay mess bills, so I was comforted by the fact that I was not getting into something I could ill afford, but of course failure in anything for me is always a bitter pill to take.

Those of us who failed returned to our regiments, and as a small consolation, I was granted four days' leave, Very welcome, the more so as it meant I would be away from Messrs Bingham and Bowers and the demanding standards.

I enjoyed those few days, just longer than my first leave after passing out. I had to be back by 2359 hours on the Sunday evening, and had decided to volunteer to join a cavalry regiment and go wherever they were stationed. In my case this turned out to be the Third Carabiniers (Prince of Wales Dragoon Guards), then serving in Osnabruck, Germany. What had I already learned about volunteering? Always go for the opposite of what you want.

Chapter Six

Permanent Staff

It might be appropriate at this point, having failed in my efforts (not very realistic) to become a commissioned officer, to mention one or two of the officers who, during my service, were a part of the 65th training regiment. The photograph overleaf was in fact taken a year later than the time we have now reached in my story but includes those who have a particular interest for me, and of whom I am going to make mention. Looking at the photograph brings back many memories, some good, others not so good, and there are one or two officers I scarcely remember.

The most obvious person with which to start is our 'celebrity', Second Lieutenant Noel Harrison, fourth from the left, back row. The son of the renowned actor Rex Harrison, Noel became a one-hit wonder with his record 'Windmills of Your Mind'. I still only associate this title with him, although others have recorded it, and I think his was the best version of all. I never met him, and do not even know what work he fulfilled in the unit, but it is nice to think we had someone famous among us.

There were two padres, one C of E, the other RC, centre right, middle row. We met these gentlemen quite frequently during basic training, but apart from church parades, I saw little of them during my later service.

Capt McDuell, and Capt Hubbard (third left, middle row, and third right, also middle row, respectively), were in charge of gunnery wing

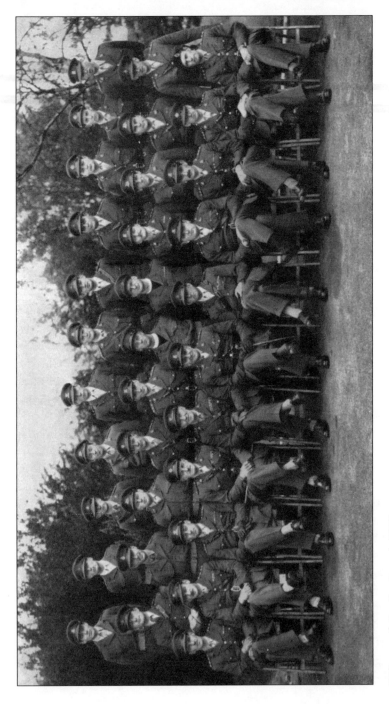

Officers of the Regiment, 1954.

and wireless wing, both based in C squadron. The former was a keen rugby player, the latter an accomplished horseman, but they both had a sense of humour and the human touch. Major Fitzherbert (distinguished in reality by a different shaped cap) and fifth from right, front row, was for some time our squadron leader in C squadron.

Lt Col Dodkins, (centre front row) was the commanding officer for the second part of my service, and wore the badges of the 3rd Carabiniers. He was a stickler for discipline, but I always found him a fair man.

Well, here I was, returning from a short leave, after having failed WOSB, and uncertain what was to happen to me. I had chosen the 3rd Carabiniers as the regiment I wished to join mainly because I admired their black webbing, unique at that time in the British army, and much easier to keep smart. The badge attracted me too. Not really very good reasons for choosing a regiment. After weeks in the Dismounted Wing, the thoughts of a couple in the Drafting Wing no longer held terrors for me, since the standards were about on a par.

The badges of the seven Cavalry Regiments we served.

49

On leaving home to return to Catterick, I promised my parents I would phone to let them know I was safely back. Since I had nowhere to go, I had to occupy a spare bed in a mixed hut that night. No, sorry to disappoint, not mixed in the sense of male and female, only in the sense of odd bods with no special duties. My bedding was also still in the stores, so I had to borrow a mattress and lie there fully clothed.

Next morning, I reported to the squadron office 'What am I supposed to be doing?'. I enquired. After a short delay, I was told I was going on leave. 'No', I said, 'I have just been on leave and returned last night.' The clerk insisted I was going on a week's leave. It appeared I had been selected to attend a more advanced radio course, but since it did not start until the next Monday, I was to go home meanwhile.

Of course I was very pleased, but still a little confused, but one does not stay and argue over going home, so back to the station I went. A travel warrant was provided, so why should I complain about travelling free on the railway? Thus it was, that just as my parents were waiting for my telephone call, I walked up the path and through the front door.

It was the following Monday, and I reported once more to the squadron office. All the news was good. First, I would be attending another six weeks' course, this time known as a cadre, being held in our regiment, but with members from all the training regiments, 65th, 66th, 67th and 68th. We were now regarded as potential instructors, and on completion (successfully) of this we would be going down to Bovington to receive ten weeks' serious and hard training to eventually become instructors. In order to go on the Bovington course, we had to be promoted to lance corporal, and now was the time to change our badges and equipment over to being members of our new cavalry regiment. There would therefore be no likelihood of being sent abroad, and we would be members of the permanent staff if we passed the course.

All this information was confirmed on the notice boards which we were instructed to read at least once every day. These also contained details of guard duties and other formal matters, but on this new course we would be exempt all duties, as we would be expected to study every evening. From our earliest entry to HM forces we were clearly instructed to read these notice boards without fail. They contained both squadron and regimental orders, and woe betide anyone who failed to carry them out. For many years after demob, I used to dream that I had failed to read orders, and had not been performing duties as instructed, waking up in the proverbial 'cold sweat' at the thought of the consequences.

To change to the new regiment, all webbing equipment now had to be washed clean of blanco, dyed black, and then polished with boot polish. The result was a smart new shine. It was still necessary to take care when shining the brasses not to get Brasso on the polish. New cap badges, collar badges and shoulder brasses had to be polished and placed in position, then all uniform jackets and greatcoats were taken to the tailor's for stripes to be sewn in place.

Except when on special courses, such as the one I was attending, we were expected to take turn on guard duty, so at this point I will give details about these rather demanding duties. There were three guards in our regiment, the Camp Quarter Guard being the one based in the main guardroom, and responsible for the regimental offices, armoury and A squadron matters. This consisted of a sergeant, a lance corporal and several troopers. Duties were either from early evening to early morning, whilst the Regimental Police were off duty, or at weekends, from midday Saturday until mid-morning on Sunday, in effect a twenty-four hour duty. The other guards were both concerned with the two tank parks, one at Hooge, the other Waitwith. Each of these consisted of a corporal, a lance corporal and nine troopers. They were for much the same timings. Main guards carried revolvers (minus firing pins), the others pick-handles, with which to tackle intruders. Whistles were also carried to raise the alarm.

At Waitwith, guards were inclined to become jumpy during hours of dark, when strange noises could be heard near to the tank hangars. These turned out to be itinerant sheep wandering in off the moor.

At Hooge, there was great competition to obtain the one beat, between 9.00 and 11.00 p. m., since this was adjacent to the WRAC living quarters and they frequently failed to draw curtains whilst they were undressing for bed. Unfortuanately, every time I was on that particular guard, I was sidetracked to doing other things and missed the show. For one man, there was a superb(?) experience. That is if you happened to fancy khaki knickers and bras!

During my time in the Dismounted Wing, I had actually performed one main guard, and one Hooge guard. The main problem was the lack of sleep, with a result that the next day you were not fully alert to what you were supposed to be doing. Troopers were allowed to sleep between tours of duty, and food was provided for all, but many found off-duty times useful for catching up on their letters home or to girl-friends. I know I did.

This cadre began, and we soon learned that there was much more to learn about wireless than we had previously thought. The six weeks should really have been ten, but since places had to be booked at Bovington, and the next course began in early August, there was only sufficient time to manage a shortened version. However, all the ground would be covered again later. There were at least three models of radio about which to learn. The WS 19 (tank set), and the WS 38, and 88, smaller personal sets. Also there would be field telephones, batteries, and other equipment. Procedures, codes, radio waves and map reading would also be covered in depth and the start of learning how to teach the subjects. Once we had grasped the basics, we would once again be taken out in lorries, specially designed to have simulated tank turrets on the back for practising communications, and giving some reality to the whole thing. We covered many miles over the North East of England, and were soon familiar with such places as Darlington, Redcar, Middlesborough, Bishop Auckland, Durham and Hartlepool.

Our instructors were all sergeants, including our old friend Len Pailing, who was still using sex to teach soldiers about wireless. We became a team, and learned how to work that way, getting to know each others' strengths and weaknesses. Most of the time the weather was kind, but if wet, we could always obtain tank suits to keep us dry.

We directed our drivers in accordance with instructions we received from the sergeants, and sometimes we would not see any other lorry for much of the day, in fact, often only when we rendez-voused for lunch break. Tea was available, and I took my water bottle (not the bed kind) to obtain my drinks. We also got to know of roadside cafes or other places where more interesting food might be found. One such place was the little back street premises somewhere in Darlington, where an elderly couple served a low priced, but nourishing beans on toast. They treated us like their own sons, and we tended to head there whenever we were in the area. No doubt they died years ago, but their kindness will always be remembered.

The main reason for these outings was for us to become familiar in the use of the tank sets. We soon discovered the usefulness, and the shortcomings in various conditions. We also learned to move position in order to improve reception. The WS 19 was intended to work over a range of between 10 and 15 miles, but we soon learned that that distance could be doubled in good conditions and reduced in bad ones. Which was what the exercises were all about, getting used to the equipment and its limitations.

Weeks flew past under this intense concentration of work, and very soon it was the end of July, and rapidly approaching the next stage of our learning. I could hardly believe that already I had completed almost a quarter of my service, though I suspected the really interesting months were still to come.

I have already mentioned that the wing was under the control of Capt Hubbard. Under his guidance the unit seemed a happy place, with everyone enjoying their work. I later discovered the added secret ingredient: the very fine method of teaching which, in my view, gave the army the edge over its civilian counterparts. Capt Hubbard's love of everything equestrian took him on a course at the army Saddle Club, in Melton Mowbray. He returned from that even more enthusiastic, and took part in local point-to-points, although he was always available when needed for the daily running of the wireless wing.

Most of us received good marks as a result of the cadre and we were ready for Bovington, resplendant in our new stripes.

Our instruction was to report to Bovington early on Sunday evening. This would allow time for settling in and meeting the other members of the class, and of course getting our bearings. A railway warrant was issued as per normal, and I was free to travel on Saturday morning. The warrant said I was permitted to travel from Darlington to Wool (somewhere I had never heard of, but I gathered it was the closest station to Bovington) via London. This would mean twenty-four hours in London, with the prospect of another overnight stop at the Union Jack club, which I did not relish. I therefore did a little 'arm twisting' with the clerk in the office, explaining that to travel via Birmingham would be both quicker and cheaper! In the end, he agreed with me and changed the authority, thus giving me part of a weekend at home. It was only six weeks since I had been home, but I did not fancy a night on an uncomfortable bed, or trying to find things to occupy my time in London. I think this was the first instance of my using my new-found rank of lance corporal.

By coincidence, Dad, who for some time had had doubts about the feasibility of the family shop for the future, had been offered a new managerial post in Redditch and was going to his first day there on the Monday.

He took me to Snow Hill station in Birmingham to catch my first train, resplendent in my new uniform, complete with stripes. There was plenty of incentive to work hard and pass this course. Not least was the threat that those failing it would lose their new-found stripes. In that case, I would most certainly have been sent to Germany, and by now, I had gone off the idea. The journey, with one change of train, took me through Southampton, where we had lived briefly when I was very small, but it was exciting to see the docks and large liners again. On arrival in Wool, the ubiquitous army lorry was there to meet the train, and take those who arrived on it the final couple of miles.

Chapter Seven

Bovington Interlude

To try to compare Bovington with Catterick would be to compare the proverbial chalk and cheese. Apart from Bovington being a camp for long-serving members of the Royal Armoured Corps, and the place where tanks were tried and tested, the atmosphere was much more relaxed than in a training unit. Buildings were much more user-friendly, food was more like eating at home, and the accommodation was much easier to keep clean. Despite the fact that it was a large military camp, the public had access to the Tank Museum, a large building which was in the same area as our billets. This meant that security was somewhat lax, although it has been tightened considerably in recent years.

After our first meal in the mess hall, certainly more appetising than anything we had seen in Catterick, we set about settling in. There were one or two familiar faces from the recent cadre but the majority of the group had completed their preliminary work some weeks before. Once more, it was a case of getting to know different people, with whom we would be working for ten weeks. We were told there would be no guard duties, or other official parades, also that we would be free each weekend from late Saturday morning, until late Sunday evening, or even in time for work on Monday morning. However, most realised that we were there to work hard and to lose a night's sleep would be inadvisable. Every evening

Accommodation huts, Bovington. Used as store (2002).

would be set aside for preparation for the next day's schedule, especially after we began to give lectures ourselves to the class. At the end of the course there would be assessments for each person, and a major examination.

Immediately after breakfast the next morning, we were taken to our classrooms, and introduced to our new instructors. I am sadly unable to recall any of their names, or even their rank, though I imagine all of them would have been sergeant or above. The syllabus of the training schedule was made known, and it soon became clear that the basis of the work would cover everything we had already been through, though in far more minute detail. Additionally, there would be the very vital teaching practices which were comparatively new to us. These were sessions where each of us in turn would be given a subject on which to lecture the remainder of the class, as if they were trainees. There would then follow an in-depth analysis of our methods and teaching ability. The instructors would be looking for thoroughness, clarity, and the handling of the classes. As we became more used to teaching, the classes were encouraged to be more awkward and pretend not to understand; we then had to overcome the difficulties.

I already had confidence that I could attain the high standard required, and I intended to work very hard in order to achieve this, thus making the most of the opportunity. I also had the impression that the others had a similar outlook. One of the things I had taken with me was a good quality hard-backed notebook into which I would enter everything from the day's lessons when relaxing in the evening. This would be completed in my neatest writing, together with illustrations of every piece of equipment we were shown. I kept that book throughout my service, using it almost daily with every class. In fact I also had it for many years beyond, only destroying it when space was at a premium during one of my house moves.

I say destroyed because although I was certain that there was nothing which had not been superseded, I did not want it falling into wrong hands. However, since my decision to publish my memoirs, I bitterly regret having got rid of something which could have jogged my memory and helped in the writing of this book.

Our efforts at teaching were recorded on audiotape, and played back to us so that we might discover the many mistakes we had made. If this had been a few years on, then there would also have been videotape which would have shown our body language, an all-important matter in personal contacts. The first time I heard my own voice on tape I was horrified. Did I really sound like that?, was it really me? There was so much to be embarrassed about in the mistakes we had made. Of course, the actual voice was unimportant except where we had placed the wrong tone or emphasis on a word or phrase, and, indeed, if we had said something incorrect. Later we overcame these problems and were much happier with our own efforts.

Apart from attending every class, the only official and compulsory attendance was a kind of roll call parade on a Saturday morning. I think this was just to ensure we had not sloped off too early, and thus had spent Friday evening consolidating the things we had been shown during the week's work. Local coaches from Bere Regis were available to take any soldiers on leave, and one of the services went direct to Worcester. They also went on a Saturday at midday. However, I only used this service once, for two practical reasons. First, the shortness of the weekend, and the length of the journey would mean only a very few hours at home. Second, and more important, was the fact that I had relatives living in Bournemouth who had kindly invited me to stay with them when I was free to do so. They kept a shop in Wallisdown which meant one short train ride, a short walk, then a trolleybus ride to get me there swiftly.

In fact, I always used to break the journey by stopping for lunch in Bournemouth, so reducing their need to feed me all weekend. This became a very pleasant routine, and often on a Sunday the visit would include a drive into the surrounding country in their car.

Sadly, the older members of that branch of the family are no longer with us, but my cousin reminds me that I caused consternation by standing at my Aunt's best table, polishing my boots rather too close to *her* polished surface. I do recall standing in my underwear, pressing my uniform trousers, though I had forgotten the matter of boots. Also, I cannot understand why I was not wearing civilian shoes instead of boots. Perhaps it was an isolated incident.

On a few Saturday evenings, my cousin invited me to join her and her friends at a local dance, and I also remember taking her to the pictures to see *Call Me Madam*, on one occasion. The return journey was usually very similar. I would be taken to the station by car to catch one of the Waterloo to Weymouth trains which stopped at Wool. These trains were full of service personnel returning from leave, Sailors going either to Poole or Weymouth, and soldiers going to Lulworth or Bovington. In those days most of the trains were steam-hauled, but once or twice we had the new diesel locos 10000 and 10001 which were being tested on the line. Of course, in those days it was quite a novelty to have these 'new' monsters hauling the train, but now times have changed and many of us would give anything to be steam-hauled again. However, that route has been largely electrified anyway.

On the one occasion I did travel to Worcester by coach, it turned out to be a foggy weekend. Most of both legs of the journey took place in really thick murk, and it was hardly worth the effort since I had only a very few hours at home.

Bovington camp was not short of facilities: there were shops, Naafi clubs, a garrison cinema and plenty of sports fields. The Tank Museum drew interested crowds at weekends or during holiday periods, with a large amount of equipment only comparatively recently having been brought there following the recent 1939–1945 war. Of course there were plenty of items from earlier conflicts. Looking at the mighty German Tiger and Leopard tanks, with their heavily reinforced steel and their large guns, it made me wonder how we ever beat them with our much smaller armour. Even the American tanks seemed small when compared with the Panzers. The first tank of any real size or gun power we possessed was the Centurion, with which our regiments were only recently equipped. Quite an advance on our previous armoured fighting vehicles. Also in the museum were badges, uniforms, and stories of valour and battles which made us proud to be part of this huge organisation. I cannot but reflect on the way in which our army has been allowed to shrink in recent years, losing many of our most historic regiments. Some call it progress!

So far as our training was concerned, in order to eliminate faults and erroneous ideas, the staff took us right back to basics, as though we had not previously learned anything. This is rather like the police, when training for Class 1 driving. Once we had mastered the theory, it was into the trucks with simulated turrets, and off into the Dorset countryside to play 'war games'. Very soon we were delighting in the names of sleepy hamlets, or bustling villages, names such as Tolpuddle, Alfpuddle, Sixpenny Handley, Tarrant Hinton, Tarrant Rushton, and many others too numerous to mention. However, there was one exercise which saw us travelling to Devon in wireless vehicles. This was concerned with skywaves – the important natural phenomenon which allows radio communications to pass round the world rather than the short distances we normally operated within. The principle of this system was to 'bounce' the signals by using the various layers round the earth. If the angle was right, then the signals could be heard many miles away. The idea of this scheme was to give us practical experience in using the various anomalies of radio communication, hopefully reaching such far away places as Hong Kong.

We set off in two elderly, fully laden lorries, each full of equipment and ourselves. We maintained only low average speeds until we reached a hill, whereupon we settled down to a speed of some five or ten miles per hour. Not surprisingly, we left trails of fuming motorists in our wake, since at that time the road between Dorchester and the Devon border was a narrow, winding, coastal route with no alternative way except those involving huge detours. Even with the levels of traffic in the 1950s, a far cry from those of today, there was much radiator and driver overheating, and not a little bad language. We would shrug our shoulders, muttering 'not our fault', then, as we breasted another hill, our weight would create the impetus to descend, outrunning most of our followers, until we reached the next upward incline, once more dragging the convoy behind us.

We spent two nights near Cullompton, on a hill site which allowed maximum local radio contact as well as the longer-distance working. Most of our wireless communication was done in the evenings, so we had some leisure in the afternoons. Local pubs stocked the famous Devon scrumpy cider, though I am uncertain whether that helped or hindered our tasks. We were very happy whilst there. We had a list of radio stations, mostly regimental ones, and we succeeded in contacting most of them. Probably the most successful was the furthest afield – Hong Kong – with Catterick quite a long way behind in quality. We must have got the bounce wrong for them. I understand that this experiment in long-distance communications was never repeated, either from Bovington or Catterick, though I am uncertain of the reason. I do not think it was because of any bad behaviour on our part, and of course in later years radio communication had improved by satellites and the like. The return journey was somewhat similar to the outward one, so there were a few dozen extra frustrated motorists in Dorset that day.

I think it would be fair to say that we all threw ourselves into the ten weeks of rigorous training with enthusiasm, but it was not all serious work; there were also plenty of laughs. One of the trickiest

Wireless set 19 on display in the Tank Museum, Bovington.

series of tasks we needed to master concerned the field telephone. This alternative method of contacting other units, especially in time of radio breakdown, was an essential part of our schedule. Instruments were connected by wire, which under some conditions would break. In battle conditions it might be broken in several places by explosives or enemy fire. Therefore, as signallers, it was vital that we learned how to effect repairs and how to use the repair kit. Soldering packs in the shape of thickened matches made of metal and with a centre portion of some type of brimstone, which had to be ignited by contact with abrasive material, were used for this. The two ends of the broken wire had to be inserted into the centre of the 'match' and held there whilst igniting the outer middle of it, a tricky manoeuvre at the best of times, requiring either two pairs of hands, or two men each with their one pair. As it would be inadvisable, under battle conditions, to have more men than necessary exposed to enemy fire, and as we were being taught to work under the worst conditions, we had to do the repair by ourselves. Wearing gloves was not possible, because of the more delicate parts of the operation. The result was much hilarity, some scorched skin, and a great deal of ripe language similar to that used by the proverbial trooper. Eventually we mastered the task, but it certainly gave us many lighter moments.

One evening after our daily training, we were informed that we had 'volunteered' for a special assignment. This was to be at nearby Lulworth, where we would be taking part in a series of important experiments within the grounds of the gunnery school. Off we went in one of the 'whistling' lorries, driven in the usual horned, tailed member of the devil's squad of B4 drivers' manner. These lads were always prepared to show off their 'skills' frightening the life out of other road users and confining old ladies to the side of the road from which they wanted to cross. On arrival (surprisingly without damage), we were issued with tank suits and ushered into a side room. Here, we were given a piece of paper to read, and, having read it thoroughly, to sign. It turned out to be a copy of the Official Secrets Act, which told us that, on pain of some quite nasty punishment, we must never reveal the things we were about to witness. What we saw that night is no longer on the secret list, since the equipment has been standard issue to the British army for some years, but I am taking no chances. We went out into the short rifle ranges, were given positions to maintain, and operated infantry radio sets to receive and then to pass on instructions.

From time to time we would be moved elsewhere, and the operation would be repeated. At the end we were treated to cocoa and toast and were driven back to Bovington, minus the tank suits, which we had found very useful.

You may be wondering whatever happened to the girl-friend I left behind me, or rather up in Glasgow. Well, a fairly regular correspondence had been conducted, plus an occasional phone call. I had not consorted with any other woman, and remained a reluctant virgin. To be honest, there had been little opportunity to go looking for anyone, even if I had wanted to. By now, she was at university, and her father was very anxious that she obtained a good degree by hard work. Thus, he was not over-encouraging in the case of our friendship. As the course progressed, I began to consider a visit to Glasgow to see her when leave was granted on passing the training successfully. There would be a break in her studies which would coincide with my leave, and so plans were made for me to visit. My journey could be broken in Kidderminster so that I would be able to visit my parents, then, before I returned to Catterick I would have four or five days to spend in Glasgow, which was a delightful prospect.

Meanwhile, back in the south, apart from what Bournemouth or Bovington had to offer, there were other local places of interest to visit, with either literary or historical interest, some with both. However, the reason for being down there was to work hard, so unfortunately I was unable to visit these sites. In fact, it is only recently that I have been able to put that omission right by going to some of them. They include Thomas Hardy's cottage down the road at Woolbridge, a pretty thatched cottage which has been isolated from heavy traffic by the closing of a small bridge and the insertion of a by-pass. A mile in the opposite direction, at the top end of the tank drives at Clouds Hill, stands another cottage. This was the home of T. E. Lawrence (of Arabia) when, in his last years, he served in the Tank Corps to try to avoid being pestered by people after his return from the Middle East. Further away lies Dorchester, the town where the infamous Judge Jeffries held court, sentencing many people harshly. This was known as the Bloody Assizes. Just North of Bovington lies the village of Tolpuddle. The Tolpuddle Martyrs were a group of labourers who fought against the unfairness of the system and its harsh conditions. They were transported overseas in the manner of the time.

Whilst I attended the instructors' course in Bovington, I learned many things that were of use not only in the remainder of my service, but also in dealing with the army and its methods. I was impressed with the manner of teaching, which was then, if not still, vastly superior to the standard in the civilian world. Especially I noticed that it produced better teachers than did the system which provided masters at my own school.

It brought out the best in all pupils, especially assisting those who were slower than the others, working to the level of the weakest rather than the strongest, though there were ways in which to ensure that anyone too far behind would be taken from the class. Teaching in the army is certainly a much fairer method, with no sarcasm to belittle students, and with instructors being firm but friendly whilst remaining in control. I consider these ways to be common sense, yet the masters I came across in my education broke every one of those rules, caused misery and even ruined young lads' future lives.

The golden days of August had given way to the misty mellowness of October, and the course was drawing to a close. We had witnessed the shortening of the days, and the weakening of the sun.

Our final week consisted of teaching and more teaching, assessment and more assessment, and final exams. I am unable to remember if anyone failed, and as we were all to shortly go our separate ways, there would soon be new people to get to know. Our abilities to teach others had been tried, tested and found satisfactory, though it had been a hard struggle at times. Much blood, sweat and tears had been shed on both sides, but I was delighted to have achieved something I valued most highly, and still remember with pride. The ten weeks had passed in the blink of an eye.

Three days later, and I was heading north from Birmingham on the mid-day Glasgow express, due to arrive around five o'clock. I was looking forward to this, my first meeting with Kirsteen for almost a year, and was delighted when she met me at Glasgow Central station in the family car. She had passed her test first time, like myself, at around the same time, but I had to acknowledge that anyone who could drive in Glasgow was capable of driving almost anywhere. We were soon sitting down to the evening meal with her family. I sensed that her father was still concerned that I might have an adverse influence on her studies, so he was somewhat cool in his manner. That may have been because he was by nature a very dour Scot. My opinion was that he showed too much concern, for Kirsteen was an industrious and committed young lady and not likely to have her head turned by outside matters.

We managed a number of outings, including a train ride to the coast at Ayr, ice hockey at Paisley Ice Rink, which I have never seen live since, and a couple of quiet meals together in the city. Something was wrong, I sensed, though I could not identify it. Inevitably we would have changed, with her having become an assured university student, and me a more worldly soldier, but things between us did not seem the same. We never put this into words, perhaps we should have, but it is way too late to worry all these years later. Having been amongst 'experienced' men for some months, my natural instincts were to push our relationship forward, but possibly I was too clumsy. Anyway, my advances beyond the kiss and cuddle stage were not appreciated, and the resulting coolness between us was enough for us both to agree there was no future. A very sad finish to what had been a lovely friendship.

Chapter Eight

Life As An Instructor

I heard later that Kirsteen had obtained a degree and was working as a teacher down in Haywards Heath, not so far from where we had first met in Eastbourne. However, complete severance meant that I never saw her again, and have no knowledge of how her life went over the intervening time to now. For many years after our parting, even after I was first married, I used to dream about my first love, and obviously wished we had kept in touch.

Well, here I was back in Catterick, waiting to begin the next stage of my service, having my own hut and shortly to meet my first crew of trainees. My hut was no. 14, and of course I now had privacy and my own coal fire. With winter approaching this would be a comfort. There had been a change since my own pass out, in that pay parade was now held at mid-day, and those going on leave could now catch their trains.

I am uncertain how long this had been in operation, because of being in Bovington to receive my own weekly amount, but certainly my new crew were able to get away on time.

I was very fortunate with my first group: they had passed out as a smart intake and came over to C squadron glowing with the need to be smart, also ready to keep their new billet bright and shining. All of which made my job as a new NCO much easier. It was just possible to complete their course prior to Christmas block leave, and they paid attention to what I had to tell them. Off we went with great enthusiasm. Naturally, I taught in the early days under the watchful eyes of the wing senior instructors, until I proved my ability both to teach and maintain discipline and to drill the squad when necessary.

I made good use of my personal note book, wherein lay most of the answers, but I remembered a sound piece of advice from my own training. If asked a question you are unable to answer, never try to bluff your way through it. Admit you are not sure, look it up, and later return to the class with the correct solution. No one knows everything, least of all someone fresh out of training, and the class respects your honesty. For a while it was necessary to make heavy use of the book, but gradually the facts were firmly planted in my mind, and the book functioned purely as a back-up.

No longer was I excused duties, even though lessons often needed to be prepared in advance. Thus my first duties as second-in-command of various guards soon began. There were also tours of duty as orderly NCO with the responsibility of waking the squadron in the mornings. I had obtained a riding crop with which to bang dustbin lids to rouse everyone.

Around this time there were some changes in the hierarchy of the regiment. The first new person to arrive was a new drill sergeant major, SSM 'Chesty' Reed. Rumour had it that his nickname evolved as a result of a wartime injury, and having a plate inserted in his back, but this was never established. Another rumour circulating about him was that he was so unpopular in the regiment in Germany that someone had tried to pin him up against a wall with a tank. However, there was no proof for this either. I was now glad that I had never gone out to the 3rd Carabiniers in Osnabruck, since, unfortunately, he was a member, and very soon proved to be a bundle of spitting fury with the intention of dragging the regiment kicking and screaming into line with the Brigade of Guards with the standard of drill. All NCOs below the rank of sergeant would be forced to attend a fortnight's drill cadre in A squadron. Chesty reckoned that this was necessary because these corporals had become slack, and their standards low. The first group to go on one of these 'hell spells' were those who currently had no classes of their own, and would otherwise now be enjoying a good 'skive'.

All those going on these courses would have to leave their own huts, and go and live in the 'spiders', a set of buildings joined onto a central ablutions block, shaped roughly like a spider. These units made it easier to control people within an area and easier also to administer punishment in the form of being confined to a single place. The standard of equipment, accommodation and drill expected from those on the course was higher even than the Dismounted Wing.

Over in C squadron, I was blissfully unaware that Chesty was spreading his net wider and wider, and would eventually include every corporal in the regiment. This, despite the fact that quite obviously he was a new broom sweeping through all squadrons. My crew had a 96% pass rate for their wireless training, which everyone seemed to consider a good start. I was well pleased. Certainly the attitude of the group had made my first teaching very easy, and I was grateful.

Meanwhile, my first crew would be going home to tell them all about the wireless course, and no doubt what they thought about their instructor. I anxiously scanned the order boards to see whether or not I would be going home too, and was relieved to discover I was.

Despite it being Christmas, I am unable to remember anything specific about the leave, except that the travelling was similar to all block leaves: bus to Darlington, train to Birmingham, and another bus back into Kidderminster. I expect that I would already have bought most of my presents to give out when I arrived back over Christmas, and that I would have met my pals, and gone to at least one dance. The rest of the time it would have been a case of visiting relatives and enjoying parties.

Once back at Catterick, it was a case of meeting my second crew and going through the same routine as before. Spare time, if any, was mostly spent either in the corporals' club, of which I was a member, or on Saturdays if not on duty, visiting Darlington and going to the pictures, and possibly also having a meal.

Corporals' Mess, 1954.

It was not such a bad life, and I could tolerate it if it continued that way.

My second class was very much like the first. They were disciplined and there was little trouble in keeping up the standard for weekly inspection and for special occasions. The only difference was that it was now mid-winter, and on schemes tank suits were necessary to keep ourselves warm. We still headed for beans on toast if we were in the Darlington area, this being much preferred to cold 'doorstep' sandwiches.

With the extra weekly pay I received as a lance corporal, I attempted to make my room rather more of a home from home. A few extra luxuries were appreciated. A radio to listen to the 'Top of the Pops' on Radio Luxembourg, a toaster, and an electric razor, but the latter failed to deal effectively with my heavy growth of beard, and I did not use it that much. On a Sunday evening when the top twenty was being broadcast, I left the room door open so that the crew could hear the tunes of the day. Our friend Guy Mitchell was still producing hits, then there was Johnny Ray, Dickie Valentine, and many others. One of the songs which was very popular in camp was 'Let's Walk Thisaway, not Thataway', which very soon was given new words that parodied our regimental location and some of its characters. They were not filthy words, I might add, so that was unusual! By the time the programme came on, lights had been turned out, so we listened in the dark. Week after week I went to sleep only to wake some time later and have to get up and switch the set off. Still, it was something which maintained our interest in outside things.

The crew did me proud, once more, with a result high in the 90–100 per cent bracket. However, before my next group could arrive, I had a date with Chesty and the Spiders. Not a pop group, but the hated drill cadre that was the scourge of the regiment. I have to admit that I reacted badly to this interruption – most of the reaction going inside myself – as I could not take it out on those in charge. I resented the wrench out of my new-found cosy little world, and found the return to severe discipline far worse than my initial basic training. Of course much more was expected of NCOs and no excuses were allowed for being below standard. I missed the power I had over others, and hated being back in the seat where it was me that was controlled. Perhaps that tells people something about myself which I hate admitting to, but it is the truth. Everything was expected to be top class, and if it was not we could expect a really rough ride. Kit was flung across the room, and had to be retrieved, got up to standard, and laid out again until it was satisfactory. No item could be out of place, and the only way we could tell our own equipment from the jumble on the floor was by the last three numbers from our identity, marked on possessions.

We were taught to shout and scream on the square, drilling the rest of the squad, and every word of command had to be clear and correct. Ironically, the screaming was reacted to more swiftly than ordinary shouting. Everyone took it in turns to put the squad through all the normal drill in turn, so you can imagine how many times we marched round the square each day. Particular attention was paid to giving the word of command on the correct foot.

Drill and kit layouts were not the only activities whilst on this horrific interlude. My least favourite activities, PT and assault courses, were also included, the latter making us filthy with mud, and necessitating our then having to clean up both equipment and barracks thereafter. I have never been an expert at any kind of physical test, and whilst in the assault course tunnels I could get quite claustrophobic. Even the shorter ones could be nerve-racking, especially if someone else was stuck either side of you, and you had to wait to get free. On our return, we would find no heat because the stoves had been 'bulled' for the next inspection. The only place to go would be the bath house. We walked over our highly polished floors in stockinged feet to prevent bringing mud on to them. Because of the intense pressures and high standards demanded, we became paranoid over the minutest little detail. All broom handles were scraped with razor blades, then polished, and anything which could be given a shine was given one.

Morale was about as low as it was possible to imagine. Yet we had to give an outward appearance that we were tough corporals, and capable of chasing young recruits whenever necessary. During this era it was noticed that all standards throughout the 65th had been raised to a new high level. We were expected to take no nonsense from those beneath us in rank, and in future all inspections over which we presided would be doubly checked to ensure we had missed nothing.

To this day, I am uncertain if Chesty's new regime was a coincidence, or had been deliberately arranged in advance of replacements for our two most senior persons in the regiment, the CO and the RSM. Whatever the truth, within a very short time, out went Colonel Allen and RSM Wood, and in their place came Colonel Dodkins and RSM Blackshaw. We all anticipated that there would be a few changes and a bit of tightening up, but then things would start to settle down to normal levels. In this, we were most sadly disappointed, and our cosy little routines were shaken badly, even after the changes installed by Chesty. Within minutes of their arrival came changes which would affect everyone with no exception. Nearly fifty years later, I remember RSM Blackshaw as someone who would not accept less than one hundred and ten per cent from every single member of the regiment, and was prepared to make life hell for everyone who failed to attain his high standards. His dislike of National Servicemen was evident and his dislike of NS senior NCOs even greater, as we will see.

At long last, the drill cadre was over and we all returned to normal duties. My nerves had returned to what passed for normal, but one thing remained: a determination not to accept anything but the best from those under my command. This turned out to be a wise decision as my next class turned out to be well below standard.

Amongst a number of friends I made in the corporals' mess was one with whom I seemed to have a good rapport. His name was Smith, or Smudge as I called him, though I never discovered his first name. His initial was F, and by coincidence we both worked in the stationery trade before we were called up, he worked in W. H. Smith, Droitwich. In the writing of this book I have attempted to find if he is still living, and in fact where he now lives, but without success, because I am certain his memories would have added to the story. However, it has to remain my personal memory.

During our spare time, we would wander round Richmond together, down along the River Swale watching ordinary folk enjoy themselves, and wishing we were back in civvy street. These kind of things made a pleasant diversion from military matters and also included the Castle, and in summer watching young people bathe in the river. We would pop into each other's quarters for a chat, and together would look forward to demobilisation.

During one of his visits to Hut 14 he noticed a peculiar smell which was strong, and getting more so. We decided that it could not be healthy, and was certainly not originating from normal sources, so it was reported to the squadron office. Within a short time, it was recognised as a real health hazard, since the smell was emanating from broken sewer pipes below the hut itself. We were swiftly evacuated to another billet, whilst a fairly extensive digging operation was commenced, and remained in that spare accommodation until the problem was rectified some weeks later.

I can remember some more names of friends, with a little help and prompting from the corporals' mess photograph reproduced here from a copy of the regimental journal of the time. They include Phil Grinyer, 'Paddy' Geraghty, John Brown, Brian Howorth, and John Blythe. Some were in C squadron, but I have had no contact with any since demob. John Brown came from Blackwell in Worcestershire, but the others were from other areas.

Every year there was a large inspection of the entire regiment, and everything concerning it. This was known as the Admin inspection and was conducted by high-ranking officers from Northern command. Everything was to be absolutely perfect, from the paint on buildings down to the grass lawns in front of most huts. For weeks before the day everyone was busy getting it all to standard. Special squads, plus all those on fatigues, would be marshalled into becoming painters, rubbish collectors, and grass cutters. If there were insufficient lawn mowers, then scissors were to be used. That's right, scissors, cutting each blade of grass individually. In 1954, the event came just a few weeks after Mr Blackshaw arrived, so we thought, at first, his over-zealousness was connected with the inspection. We were wrong! So far as cutting the grass was concerned, we might well have collected a flock of sheep from the moors and let them loose, but then we would have had to clear up their droppings later.

My promotion to full corporal was now through, giving me that extra bit of authority and power, since lance corporals could not place people under arrest. It also brought me the job of guard commander on the tank park guards.

The new regime which had been established from the drill cadre included two separate inspections before every function where best uniforms were used. Guard-mounting parades, late night parades, guards of honour for visiting persons etc. The regimental orderly corporals were responsible for the first of these inspections and, after examining everything minutely, had to take details of and report anyone below standard. Failure to do this resulted in that corporal being in serious trouble, so to ensure self preservation, every one was doubly pernickety over standards. Since the guard were all

Myself as a newly promoted corporal and my late mother.

usually raised from the same squadron, all duty NCOs were involved, then subsequently inspections were carried out by the duty sergeant major and the duty officer, so we all held our breathe that no slight blemish had been overlooked. The buck was passed all the way down the line, as is usual in military units, with the poor trooper in this instance being left with shit on his head coming from the proverbial fans with much force.

The war in Korea was virtually over, but it was still a place to send consistently bad soldiers as a severe punishment, rather like German soldiers during the last war being sent to the Russian front. In winter, Korea was almost as cold as Russia, and was to be avoided at all costs. A cartoon in the regimental journal suggested that our new CO had a direct hotline to Korea, but that was probably an exaggeration.

Mr Blackshaw's tactics must have paid off, since there were no adverse reports after Admin, so things soon returned to the new level of normal.

I have mentioned that it was at this time I had my first (and fortunately only) bad squad. With all the increase in standards over in A squadron, I never understood how they were allowed to pass out, but when they arrived in C squadron they were generally scruffy, certainly untidy, and disobedient in relation to given orders. The serious state of their equipment and uniforms was only discovered at the first squadron leader's weekly inspection. Prior to that it was assumed they could only have passed out if up to standard. At the inspection kit was thrown around, some of the items on the huts inventory were put outside, and I was in trouble due to the men being my responsibility. A second inspection was ordered for two days later, and I was left in no doubt that the standard was to be raised considerably, or else. Once the inspectors had left, I kept the squad by the side of their beds, and explained in words of clear Anglo-Saxon that no one would be allowed out of the hut except for training until I was satisfied that everything had been put right. That included NO Naafi break or any other reason for being absent. I was not going to take the rap for this idle, scruffy, undisciplined shower, whatever it cost them

When I checked on the work and the squad during that evening, I discovered two men had left the hut, despite my clear instructions.. They obviously thought my bark was worse than my bite. At this time, Smudge was just on his way in to see me, and as he mounted the steps I was in full flow again. I heard him say to one of the chaps 'What did you say?', and he told me that the person had softly muttered under his breath, 'Balls', after I had made a specific point. I had that man marched to the guardroom, then went looking for the missing two. When I found them in the Naafi I put them on a charge at once, which meant I had three members of the squad up before the squadron leader next day. They were all given tough punishments and from that moment on the standard of all improved dramatically, and they passed all subsequent inspections. They achieved quite a good result at the end of their trade training, so my toughness had proved effective. Had they been allowed to get away with things, they would have had an extremely nasty shock when entering the Drafting Wing, so it did them a favour.

Corporals were considered the ideal rank to send out on escort duty. That is, to collect someone who had been AWOL from another barracks or out of police custody. They would be brought back to stand trial, but it was up to the regiment to collect them from whatever custody they were held in. Often, these duties took place at weekends, thus not affecting normal routine, and they could be to anywhere in the country. Usually the corporal took one trooper with him, unless the prisoner was known to be, or expected to be, violent or likely to try to escape once more. Handcuffs were carried, and on arrival at the station for the return journey, it was necessary to see the RTO (rail transport officer) to obtain an empty compartment. I am not certain whose feelings we were supposed to be shielding, the prisoner's or the public's.

If you were available, you could be sent out on escort at any time, regardless of train times, meal times or anything else. That explains why on at least one occasion, I found myself on a station, there being no train for several hours, trying to sleep in the most uncomfortable situation, an example being on the top of the table in the waiting room of Darlington station. My three escort duties were to Falkirk, Manchester and Worcester. The latter coming on a Bonfire Night as a pleasant surprise. Needless to say, I managed an overnight stop at home. However, one had to be careful not to be away too long on such duties, as you will see from this little tale.

A corporal from the Wireless Wing, also a friend since he lived not too far from home, Jerry Webb, was sent down to London to collect a prisoner from Old Scotland Yard. On arrival, he found that the man was one of his former pupils, who had gone absent for domestic reasons. Jerry decided that not only did he not need the handcuffs since the chap was willing to accompany him, but also that they could enjoy an hour or two in the city. Perhaps he had a rush of blood to the head, or possibly he just did not think properly, but the chump decided to take the prisoner to see the nudes at the Windmill theatre.

The escort had been considered straightforward, and their return was anticipated swiftly due to the wide choice of trains back to Darlington from King's Cross, so as the time passed the regimental watchdogs made urgent enquiries and found that the man had been collected from Scotland Yard. A hue and cry ensued. When they returned to camp Jerry was put on a charge, and after due process of military law, he was reduced to the rank of trooper. For the remainder of his service, he served as a clerk in the squadron stores.

Fortunately my escorts were without incident, and I returned with the prisoner when I should have, or at least within an acceptable time of what was expected. Perhaps I was just fortunate enough to know how far to bend the rules.

Chapter Nine

Dust to Dust

Whenever anyone regarded as top brass visited the regiment a special Guard of Honour was assembled, with all its members being drawn from the same cavalry regiment, one of the seven which we served. All were members of the permanent staff, wearing the same badges, thus giving an appearance of uniformity. In best uniforms with shining equipment, they paraded outside the guardroom, where they were inspected by the Adjutant and the RSM. Between them, these men would miss nothing, so it paid to be absolutely on the ball. I was fortunate enough never to have been involved in any of these stressful occasions, so avoided Mr Blackshaw at his most severe.

I took my duties as orderly NCO very seriously, especially in regard to making preliminary inspections prior to guard mounting. In fact self-preservation had turned me into a right bastard. Everyone knew which corporals were to be feared on these occasions, and to illustrate this I tell the following story against myself. One day when the guard was being provided by C squadron, I happened to be walking through two of the huts. I overheard the following conversation. 'Who is duty corporal tonight?' 'Corporal Kettle.' 'Oh my gawd!'

Of course, when I was out with my own crews I was much more relaxed, and as a result, not only did they learn well, but we had some pleasant days out. In the same way that I had first travelled round many of the interesting areas of the north east, I took them to many of those areas, so the crews too became familiar with places that earlier in their lives had been merely names on a map. Of all the towns visited during my two years service, only Harrogate, Ripon and Bedale have been revisited by me since leaving the army. They had hardly changed over the years, and it was nice to be able to visit with more time to enjoy them.

All this time I was not getting much driving practice, and I had for some time wanted to try driving a small army truck. Although it was strictly unofficial, and definitely against the rules, I pulled rank sometimes whilst out on schemes to get the drivers to allow me to drive when conditions and circumstances made it safe to do so. I discovered that the lorry was much different to handle from even a large car, and I made certain that I only took the wheel for short periods. Of course, it was never during the actual exercise, as I had to be directing operations and could not manage both jobs. So far as I am aware, no one ever found about about these little escapades, although by coincidence I was later detailed to a job where it was necessary for me to drive a Land Rover. However, that was just like a car in substance.

Despite my enjoyment in teaching recruits all about wireless equipment and operation, I never refused a chance to get away from Catterick for a while. My view of the camp was that it was depressing, and not the best place in the world to be, so I was ever willing to volunteer for external assignments, despite my caution over the experience of volunteering, and in any case this new work was thrust on me without a chance to say no.

A large national military exercise was to take place across Salisbury Plain, of several days duration, and one of the umpires, a senior Brigadier, required a driver/wireless operator to accompany him throughout the whole scheme. Presumably because of my radio experience, and not through my illegal driving, I was chosen for the task. First I had to obtain the vehicle from a neighbouring regiment, the Fifth Royal Iniskilling Dragoon Guards (known familiarly as the Skins), although I never discovered why one of our own regimental Land Rovers could not have been used. Together with others in a small convoy, which included a large slow and lumbering Humber staff car and other vehicles, we set off in the early dawn to drive at a tedious forty miles per hour, all the way to Larkhill, an Artillery depot in the centre of the plain, a considerable distance. We had already breakfasted on our cookhouse's famous fried egg sandwiches, and made two further stops for food and drink on the way. Apart from getting hopelessly lost in the middle of Leicester, due to the lack of signposts showing the route we required, and also experiencing some petrol feed problems with my vehicle, the trip was uneventful. However, thirteen hours behind the wheel, especially at one speed, led to drowsiness among all of us. Certainly I was beginning to nod by the time we reached Larkhill.

There could be no question of stopping anywhere overnight, since with typical army planning, which left very little spare time, and the scheme due to commence promptly next morning, there was only just enough time to prepare the vehicles and have a meal and a few hours' sleep. We were certainly relieved to find our quarters and get to bed.

Our instructions had been very lacking in detail, especially concerning what was to happen the next morning. After breakfast I set out for the officers' mess, where I arrived with time to spare before meeting Brigadier Whetstone. One of the little details omitted from our orders was that we should draw haversack rations from the cookhouse each day. They would only have been sandwiches, but the lack of food could have been very much a problem. Fortunately the Brigadier, sensing my predicament and discomfort, and without sufficient time to return for anything, offered to share his food with me, an offer I accepted with alacrity. The only time in my life I have eaten pheasant sandwiches, and very nice they were too, as was the small bottle of lager he happened to have spare. This was a typical example of my opinion that the higher in rank, the easier the communication, and the more pleasant the person. I thought he seemed young for this high rank, and he was certainly pleasant to work with. He did, however, very quickly decide that he would like to do most of the driving, leaving me with the radio operation, a division of labour that worked very well throughout the exercise.

During the next few days we covered many miles over the Plain, both on roads and various open areas of grassland and dust. It was very warm and dry, so there were only odd patches of mud. We passed several times through the former village of Imber, long since out of bounds to civilians, and now a target and practice area for artillery and tanks. There was a fair amount of night driving, travelling along narrow lanes with only the tiny lights on the rear axle of the vehicle in front to follow. This meant driving close to the one ahead and keeping up whatever speed they were doing. There were ditches on either side of the main track, and I was very pleased not to have been driving.

During the scheme, HRH The Duke of Edinburgh flew in by helicopter to check on the happenings, although we did not see him. Tanks were chasing at great speed, creating huge columns of dust, and I assumed they were mostly Centurions, then the main battle tank of the British army.

At the end of the exercise the convoy returned to Catterick, but by a different route. We travelled by way of Evesham, where we had a brief stop, frustratingly close to home, with no chance of diversion. The Land Rover, which had been under my signature throughout the period, behaved itself so far as the petrol problem was concerned. Despite a few nail-biting moments, there was not a scratch on the vehicle when I handed it back and breathed a sigh of relief. Bring on the next crew!

You will have gathered that Catterick was not top of the popularity stakes, so far as most of the thirty thousand garrison inmates were concerned. However, it had to be said that it had many facilities, comparable with most towns of similar size. In the area known as Camp Centre, for obvious reasons, were the huge Naafi Club, complete with dance hall and several bars, also restaurants. There were also some small shops. Around other parts of the garrison were churches, a large cinema (The Essoldo), swimming pool, golf course and riding facilities. So far as the dance hall was concerned, it had to be said there was not a great deal of dancing. With the ratio of men to women of around twenty to one, you can realise the average chap had little chance of getting a dance. In fact I never knew anyone who did. Most of the females who went there were in the WRAC and my impression was that a bloke had to have a very special line in chat-up before getting any of them interested. I can only imagine what attributes a man required before achieving success with one of these khaki-knickered Amazons. A mere inexperienced virgin like myself had no chance. So I never even tried.

The camp had its own railway station with one platform, so it was mainly used for trains bringing lads and lassies back at weekends. Access to this branch line was off the Richmond branch, which meant a certain amount of engine shunting to go through the various changes of direction. My own experience of it was on Monday mornings, usually around 4.00 a.m., often in the cold, at the end of a journey which had begun from New Street around 10.00 p.m. the previous evening. We remained in the same carriages, leaving the British Rail engines to get us over the various points. These trains were normally packed with snoring soldiers, not happy to be returning to camp, being told off by the ticket collectors for removing the light bulbs so that we could sleep in peace. On dismounting from a warm compartment we were faced with a choice between a longish cold walk, or a taxi we could ill afford, most of us chose the walk to save the few pennies we had left, although on a snowy winter's morning we were tempted to jump into a cab. Often that cab was full to overflowing to try to keep down the individual fare.

Military units like the army dental corps were also located in camp centre, as I discovered when in agony with teeth into which had blown the cold winds from the Antarctic wastes. I had been told that army dentists were 'butchers', and by the time I reluctantly used their services I was ready to leave without treatment. Because the pain was excruciating, I was glad to go eventually, and very relieved to find out that, in fact, they were very gentle indeed. I took little persuasion to go back for a second extraction later Having received deadening injections, I discovered that eating lunch afterwards could be quite a tricky business, spilling half my soup while trying to locate my mouth.

My duties as guard commander were not unduly arduous, apart from the loss of sleep. I carried out duties at both Hooge and Waitwith, though not at the same time, I might add. Those tours lasted twelve hours, as the tank hangars were in constant use most days, and it was only our task to ensure no one roared off down the road at the helm of these fifty-ton monsters. Apart from checking on the sentries at various times throughout the night, most of the corporal's work consisted of detailing people to collect food and drink, and making out reports. Other than sheep wandering in from the moors at Waitwith, and the hope of seeing the WRACs undress at Hooge, there were few disturbances. Some of the young lads who had not previously done guard duty needed reassurance, especially when confronted with a sheep only interested in chewing the grass, and making a certain amount of noise doing it.

At around the middle of 1954, one of the members of a squad in training enquired if I would be interested in writing to a girl who was one of his neighbours, and who wanted a soldier to write to. She lived in Harold Hill, Essex, and I am pretty certain that the enquiry was passed to me either as a bet, or because someone was trying to take the micky, but I decided it might be fun. After all I had no girl to write to now. This girl's name was Jean, and she was a couple of years younger than me. During the correspondence she seemed a pleasant young person. She was a typical teenager of the 1950s, keen on Dickie Valentine, interested in music, dancing, tennis and the usual pastimes. Our letters showed that we had quite a lot in common, and I decided I would like to meet her. Somehow, her parents were persuaded to invite me to stay one weekend, so I decided to spend my next seventy-two hour pass with the family. My parents were horrified that I was going to a home and family I had never met, and on reflection I suppose it was rather risky for all of us.

However I was determined to give it a whirl, and so arranged to stay down there.

For the first, and last, time going on leave, I boarded a train for King's Cross, and from there transferred to Liverpool Street where I caught the connection to Harrold Hill. I found that they lived in a nice area in a pleasant semi-detached house, complete with small garden. Jean and her parents turned out to be very nice people, and I was soon being treated like one of the family. The only awkward situation was caused by Jean having an elder brother and there being only three bedrooms. This meant my sharing with that brother, except that on my day of arrival he was out late, so we did not meet until next morning, although we shared the same bed. The visit was a success. We had pleasant days, including a visit to London's West End, and we played tennis in a local park. I did get a little keen on her, but as her Dad pointed out, she was very young, and advised that I did not get too serious. Sound advice, since our correspondence faded after a little while, and we never met again. At that age two years' difference, especially with me being in the army, was rather more important than it would be now. I had to agree that the experiment had been rather risky, although in the event, no harm was done.

On entry into the forces, we were given this instruction. 'If it moves salute it, if it does not move, pick it up, and if you can't pick it up, paint it white.' No doubt this remains the standing order it has been for many years. My sense of humour wondered whatever would have happened if an officer was standing very still when one saw him!! Fortunately, as far as I know, the matter was never put to the test.

With the job of teaching wireless now firmly in my grasp, I instigated some new exercises for my crews to add to their interest. We still went out in the lorries using the WS 19 tank radios, but now I also began ground exercises on the local moors with the smaller infantry radios, still practising our communication skills. They gave the lads a new interest and a different set of circumstances, and they seemed to respond well to this new addition..

When I tell people that I served in the Royal Armoured Corps, everyone imagines the glamour of always working inside tanks. Sitting in the turret of a large Centurion tank, complete with headphones, and communicating with other similar units is uppermost in their minds. I regret to admit that the truth is rather less romantic, I only went inside a tank once, and that in somewhat unromantic

Centurion Mk 3 tank, Bovington Tank Museum.

circumstances. Some person who has to my knowledge never been identified, had a 'clever' idea. Wouldn't it be exciting to use one of these huge tanks to get rid of some of the old married quarters, bungalows which had outlived their usefulness? Would it not also be exciting to persuade a couple of idiots, a signaller and a driver, that they would find this an exhilarating experience? I had no reason to think that both the idea and the fact that I allowed myself to be talked into this daft idea had doubtful qualities.

Two of us, the driver and myself, entered our respective compartments and closed the hatches. Radio communication was established and the orders were passed. With my tannoy set, I passed the instructions to the driver. Start up the engine, reverse to a point which would allow a good run at the building, then let her go. We hit the bungalow at around twenty miles per hour, fast enough for the impact to be quite hard. There was a terrific crash, and the vehicle shuddered to a halt, dust coming inside through every tiny access. The loudest part of the noise had been the chimney falling across the engine cover, though what with the dust and the shock of the impact we only realised this later. From the language coming from the driver's compartment, it was evident that plenty of dust had found its way there too, and that his body had been jarred by the impact. Fortunately I had been hanging on to the gun breech, and had been able to absorb much of the shock that way. We were both in one piece, and began to prepare to get out. I was unable to move the turret, it seemed to be set in concrete and would not move even one inch. Trapped! Some claustrophobia set in, not to say panic. I had no idea what to do, and it was obvious that I could not escape the conventional way. At length, a voice in my headsets suggested trying to follow the driver out of his hatch. I crawled with great difficulty from the main crew area into the driver's place and, with even more squeezing, out of the driver's hatch. Had I had my sense of humour at that moment, I would have likened the situation to when Pooh Bear had eaten too much honey, and could not get out of the rabbit hole he had earlier used to get into the warren. I later discovered that no one really believed it was impossible to escape through the main hatch, but on inspection the reason became clear. Solid wooden roof timbers had passed through spaces at the top of the hatch preventing it from opening. In so doing, very expensive periscope prisms used by the tank commander in battle conditions had been smashed.

The building had been truly demolished, but the tank was also a victim of the encounter. Only superficial damage to the front of the vehicle, and the engine was unaffected by the chimney crashing over the covers, but the turret and prisms would have been very costly to repair and replace. I would like to have been a fly on the wall at the enquiry as to how the tank came to be so damaged. Strangely, this experiment was never repeated, and I was not sorry never to be inside a tank again.

Chapter Ten

The Perils of Being an Only Son

I was nineteen and a half years of age, still a 'virgin soldier' and frustrated by both lack of opportunity and its consequent lack of experience. The WRACS and the Naafi girls seemed prepared to go out on dates, but I never asked, mainly due to the fear of ridicule and rejection. My fears were that they would only be interested in experienced men. I still regarded marriage as something special, therefore not even thinking of any liaison with one of the wives of a regimental member. To be honest, I never saw one I fancied. My close encounters with girls back home were limited by lack of suitable places to take them and by their fear of getting pregnant. Knowing my luck, I think that Sod's Law would have decreed that would have happened on any first real encounter. So I was doomed to having to wait for some months to come, getting more frustrated by the hour, especially after hearing of exciting happenings with other lads.

That frustration found its way into using food as a substitute for sex, and it resulted in an increase in my food consumption, then my weight. Whenever I went into Darlington, I would have a meal, then bring back a few more delicacies to eat in camp. No doubt this formed the basis of my bad eating habits, leading to the diabetes which developed in my thirties and which I now find rather limiting.

There can be little doubt that my strict upbringing, and the over-anxiety of both parents helped to create the lack of sexual experience too. Whenever one of my leaves coincided with a holiday my parents planned to take, I was discouraged from returning home on my own. In fact, they insisted that I join them wherever they were headed, even though it was often very inconvenient for me to be accommodated also. I could cook and look after myself, but this was not acceptable to them. Very often, these arrangements were made at very short notice indeed. My worst experience happened at the Yorkshire resort of Scarborough where I ended up sleeping for two nights in a BATH. How humiliating and how uncomfortable. It made me resolve to do something really daring just to show them, As always the plan backfired leaving me with egg on my face.

My opportunity came from the fact that there was an attractive young lady staying in the hotel She agreed to my invitation to go out walking. On the final day of my leave, we went out again before I was due to catch a train back to camp. This time we found ourselves on a deserted cliff top, ideal for what I had in mind. I had everything set up, and was making good progress when I noticed the time had passed very swiftly. It always does when you are enjoying yourself. There was insufficient time left to make this my first real experience, in fact it was now going to be a race to get back to collect my things, and rush to the station. To make things worse, we had difficulty in finding our way to the hotel, and it ended with my having only a few minutes left. I barely had time to say cheerio to my parents, and certainly not enough to get this young lady's address. I had deliberately tried to get laid in order to punish my parents, but again it was me who lost out.

Sundays in the army were very quiet, especially after the hurly-burly of normal routine. If not on duty, most of the day was spent lazing around and reading newspapers, especially if it was not nice enough for a walk. Sunday newspapers were delivered to the squadrons by a man on a bike, carrying the papers in a small truck which he towed behind. We knew where and when he could be found, and were usually waiting for him. On one Sunday I went out and waited for him. Not only was he nowhere to be seen, but no one else seemed to be waiting for him either. It eventually dawned on me that the clocks had been put back one hour, and I had forgotten to alter my watch. It was, of course, late October. Nowadays I always change all my clocks and watches on the previous evening, leaving little to chance. I seldom read papers now, they are always full of gloom and doom and I only want them for the crosswords. How life has changed.

Being in Yorkshire, despite the forbidding appearance of Catterick and some immediate surroundings, had some compensations. There were beautiful places to visit, such places as Aysgarth Falls, Castle Bolton, Fountains Abbey, Northallerton, Pickering, Swaledale and Thirsk. Most were within reasonable travelling distance, but the public transport was rather lacking, even in those days. Some of my friends had motorbikes (remember Coronation Day?), one of these being John Brown, he who hailed from Blackwell. Despite my fear of riding pillion, I knew that this would be the only way to visit these places, so I agreed to go with John, first as a test, later because I really wanted to see the sights. He showed much patience, and we managed to complete our tours without incident.

As a corporal, my pay was rather more than when I first arrived, in fact I was able to have sufficient to live on, and to send some home to be saved for the future. It was put into a building society. I often went to the cinema two or three times a week; there were plenty from which to choose. We had our own squadron cinema, there was the Essoldo at camp centre, and two or three places in Darlington. There was also one in Richmond. This was the new era of technology for the cinema, widescreen, cinemascope, even three dimensional experiments. There were adventures with Errol Flynn or Tony Curtis, adventure films concerning the 'cold war' such as *Hell and High Water*, with Richard Widmark and Bella Darvi, and also musicals with Mario Lanza and Catherine Grayson or Doris Day. So much to watch and to lose oneself in away from military reality. My romantic nature came to the fore, and I actually considered the world of cinema as real life. I was following my Dad's love of things theatrical and romantic, but it could just have been that to believe this was real was an easy way through life. Whatever the reason, I discovered the hard way that life is not a dream, more of a nightmare.

I began to take an interest in the squadron football matches, first helping to obtain kit and book pitches, then starting to referee some of the games. I even studied the rules so that I could enable the games to be fair as well as enjoyable. It was all friendly competition, nothing at stake, and I eventually became a passable controller. We all enjoyed the fun and exercise. Anyway it was better than standing on the touchline shouting at everyone in general, and at the referee in particular.

On looking back at a reasonably successful National Service career in wireless instruction, I am quite amazed at what I achieved, especially since I have never been particularly technically minded, and it meant learning a totally new form of activity. Despite the natural resentment at the interruption of one's civilian career, I had been determined to make the best of the situation and somewhat immodestly I have to say that I did just that.

The thought of one subject which did scare me when I was told that it would form a part of the course, was Morse code, but fortunately it was never mentioned again, and I never had to learn it. Though it had been used widely during the war, by the time I was called up its use was largely discontinued. The equipment was much in evidence but I never recall anyone using it. Plain voice communication was the form of radio contact in normal use throughout my service, although there were other codes which were intended to keep certain data secret. Morse was in universal use for many years, and was known to most countries, so it would hardly have been secure. Codes were intended to prevent one's positions and intentions becoming known to the enemy, and those in regular use were included in my little notebook.

Batteries, too, were very important as a subject, since much of the radio use depended on them. In a tank, they were part of the vehicle's equipment, but in lorries and the classroom they had to be dragged about from place to place, and they were quite heavy. We had to be aware of their maintenance and reasons why they failed, if that happened. To learn about these things we also had to know how batteries were made, and how various components needed to be treated.

I have already mentioned that the warmth in my own small room came from a coal fire, whilst the main stove in the hut was fuelled by coke. The coke stove ran better if started with coal. Sometimes one or both commodities were in short supply, and often before an inspection the stove could not be lit to avoid it being messed up at the wrong time. In winter, with a fresh easterly wind blowing off the moors and snow filtering through the ventilators high up on the end walls, it could be extremely cold. There were times when I opened my door to add my meagre warmth to whatever there was in the main billet, but otherwise my door was closed, and it became cosy in there.

Friends would visit, and we would often spend time putting the regiment, the country and the world to rights. Needless to say, the language could be quite colourful, and punctuated with words I prefer not to use these days. During one of my more vociferous and profane moments, there was a knock on the door. As I opened it, I saw a sergeant of the Royal Amy Education Corps standing there. At first I failed to recognise him, but then I saw that he was the son of friends of my parents, recently posted to Catterick and calling to find me. He could hardly have missed the torrent of language whilst standing outside, which made me rather embarrassed – you see, his father happened to be a Methodist Minister. He was the soul of tact, and the matter was never mentioned, but I think that after that incident I was a little more careful in my choice of words.

Bad language in the army, was, and is, normal practice. Very few trainees ever reacted immediately to orders unless reinforced by expletives to emphasise the importance of what was being communicated,

I always felt that the creators of *Dad's Army* were extremely clever in making John Le Mesurier's character, Sergeant Wilson, a person who gave orders in a quiet voice, and frequently had to be told to put more strength behind his orders. He almost apologised for telling the squad to do this or that.

Although I did meet some sergeants who left the bullying and swearing to their corporals, most of them were forceful characters. Our RSM had illustrated just how unpleasant a warrant officer could be, but drill sergeant majors such as RSM Britten of the Guards could reduce a whole regiment of soldiers to quivering jellies in moments. He was reputed at the time to have one of the loudest voices in the British army, and fear spread throughout any unit he was reported to be planning to visit. There was a time when we had a drill sergeant from the Guards helping our regiment with their drill, but fortunately I managed to avoid him.

As a schoolboy, and later, I was brought up to read plenty of books. In fact I have always enjoyed a good read, whether it be provided by famous literary people or by popular authors. My visits to new towns frequently included a browse around W. H. Smith's, Menzies, or other bookshops. On one such visit into Smith's in Darlington, I noticed the 1000th Penguin being displayed. The title was *One of Our Submarines* and it was the wartime story of a submarine commander and his experiences. I bought it, have read it many times, and I still have the book today. Perhaps it was my interest in such autobiographical writings which encouraged me to write this story, who knows?

The basic syllabus of the radio trades' course never varied, but a diligent instructor could always find new ways to put over the material to his class. I had already added the use of personal radios as a means of assisting in learning communication and its various idiosyncrasies, so now I placed a new emphasis on the subject of map reading. I had always found the subject fascinating and experience had taught me the value of proper interpretation of map signs and symbols. A few initially thought this new teaching to be a waste of time, but my enthusiasm and the detail I taught had them realising how vital this was. I am very fortunate in having a very good sense of direction. I can visit a new place, even in another country, and within a short time can find my way around. There have been times when I have even been asked for, and given directions in European towns. Although it is undoubtedly a gift, the guideline is, always look for outstanding landmarks, e.g. tall buildings, churches or the like, as soon as you arrive, and look for those things when trying to return to the starting point. Read the names of streets and squares, then look at the map to fix their position in relation to the surroundings. I was brought up with the maxim 'There is no such word as can't', and although I sometimes have great doubts about this being true, having learnt such an unlikely subject, perhaps it might be.

Bad weather rarely interfered with the training schedule, because we had warm clothing, vehicles and drinks, so I cannot recall ever cancelling an exercise. Marching on snow or ice, however, could be tricky.

We were told to march on our heels, digging them well in to the ice or snow. Despite all of us having metal tips and heels on our boots, I never remember a bad fall.

Officially our trade was signaller/gunner, so most squads, after completion in the wireless wing went over to the gunnery wing for another few weeks of training.

I had now been in the army for eighteen months, and I had forgotten most of the lads who had been in the same intake. By now, they were probably scattered around the world. Units of the cavalry were in Germany, North Africa, Hong Kong and Korea, but at least one regiment was in the UK. Some would now be bandsmen, or in one of many trades. Anyone who either had been a successful sportsman prior to call-up, or who had shown prowess in a particular sport since call-up, was given encouragement to pursue their interest. They were given every encouragement plus all the facilities available, and in some cases they became world-class in their particular field.

Rumours had been circulating for some time that one or two corporals might be in line for promotion to sergeant. Although I never really believed this would affect me, nevertheless I kept an eye on the regimental order's board. It was November 1954, and on returning from exercise one day, I was advised to look at orders. I had been promoted. What a panic, Immediately I had to move lock, stock and barrel into sergeants' mess quarters, where I must now live. I could no longer eat in the normal mess hall, only in the sergeants' mess. All my uniforms and greatcoat had now to go to the regimental tailor for alteration. All this had to be completed within hours, and once more I was shaken out of a very peaceful little rut.

Chapter Eleven

Sergeant's Stripes

One minute I had been a corporal in charge of a hut full of trainees, and responsible for their every move as well as teaching them about wireless, the next I was uprooted and transferred to the sergeants' mess where life would be much more formal. I still continued to teach, but in all other respects my life in the forces had undergone a major change. All sergeants were expected to attend official functions in the mess in dress uniform if you possessed it, although of course I had only normal uniform. It was an unwritten rule that each of us support the organisation by drinking socially in the bar during off-duty periods. My new rank was 'acting', in other words I wore the rank, had the authority, and performed all the duties of a sergeant, but was still only paid as a corporal. This presented few problems. As an almost non-drinker, I usually made one, or at the most two, drinks last all evening. I was not keen on beer, and so raised a few eyebrows by drinking a double gin topped up with ginger beer. The adverse comments on my non-drinking habits soon faded, and I was accepted for myself.

Only a few days after my promotion an official dinner was held in the mess, chaired by the senior warrant officer, the RSM. This included speeches and loyal toasts, and we were served sherry as the toasting drink. Now I had never encountered sherry before, although I knew of its existence, and I was not prepared for the consequences of drinking it too fast. A massive choking fit for a short while made me realise it needed to be taken in sips.

I learned very quickly that, after promotion, the army gives new duties very swiftly, usually with a minimum of guidance on how to perform them. A baptism of fire, so to speak. In the centre of the garrison was a large military hospital, part of which was the psychiatric wing which catered for the sick in mind, real or imaginary, the latter often being considered the way to be thrown out of the army. Such patients tried to persuade the authorities that they were mentally unbalanced, and in so doing were not unknown to end up going a little crazy. All inmates of this wing had to be kept secure, under guard, and each regiment had to take turns in providing a guard at weekends, thus it was a twenty-four hour duty.

My first duty as a sergeant was as guard commander of the hospital guard. Winter arrived early in 1954 at Catterick, so our duties were carried out with a background of several inches of snow. Those actually on duty outside were glad when their two-hour stint was over, and they could get a hot drink or meal.

The food was collected at regular intervals and kept hot for those on actual sentry go. The tasks were not specially arduous, but the commander was expected to keep awake throughout the complete guard.

I had to check on all guards at regular intervals, but fortunately the duty passed without incident, and by Sunday afternoon, we were very glad to be relieved by others.

The act of dropping me in at the deep end, however, was not yet complete, and it was only a few days later that my name was once more on the duty roster, this time as commander of the main Camp Quarter Guard. Once more it was a weekend (twenty-four hour) stint. I never discovered how one's name was chosen for duty, whether someone stuck a pin in the list, or even if it were more sinister: that someone who did not like you was being vindictive. It was very easy to become paranoid over getting a second twenty-four hour guard so quickly after the previous one, but in all probability it was mere coincidence. The only thing I do know is that this second duty was to become far more traumatic than I could ever have imagined. I almost lost my stripes more swiftly than I received them.

We paraded at mid-day on the Saturday, just when all those off duty were leaving camp to visit nearby towns or other destinations. The usual close scrutiny of all guard members took place, and we marched to the guardroom where we took over from the regimental police. We had to sign for all equipment and ensure that everyone was familiar with the standing orders about conduct and how to deal with most events. I allotted the men their duties and we settled down for another long weekend. That evening there was a massive booze-up in the corporals' mess, and in order to score some 'brownie points' the mess president had invited senior non-commissioned ranks, including the RSM. However, the afternoon was uneventful.

During the mess do, various sycophantic members were taking the opportunity to ply the RSM with drinks which were to add to his normally difficult nature. He was a small man in stature, and had only one eye, but with that, he never missed a thing. I think, on reflection, we should have called him Cyclops, but I doubt if anyone ever dared call him anything except Sir. Making up with aggression what he lacked in stature, he disliked National Servicemen in general, and where one of these persons had been promoted into the ranks of senior NCOs, he felt only grave doubts over their abilities. All this was, of course, unknown to me, which was possibly providential, but I did not remain in ignorance for much longer.

Not long after we had settled down for the night, following defaulters and late guard parade, he turned up at the guardroom door, somewhat the worse for drink, but with an increase in aggressive attitude.

I had assumed, rather naively, that once he was ensconced in the corporals' mess with a pint in his hand, he would forget about guards and suchlike, but nothing was further from the truth. Here he was, large as life, and twice as dangerous.

On being admitted to our presence, the first thing he demanded was to see the prisoners. There were two, locked in cells just along a kind of verandah from the guardroom, so I grabbed the keys and took him along to see them, unlocking the door for him to see that they were still there. Knowing that it was a courts martial offence to lose a prisoner, I locked the door behind him after he had entered. He banged on the door, fuming with rage, and on leaving the cells he told me that they might have killed him. There were to be times in the next couple of days that I was to wonder if that might have been less stressful for everyone, particularly me. We returned to the main guardroom where he proceeded to find fault with everyone and everything, although it had to be said that he was hard pressed to find anything really wrong with the set-up. We all stood to attention during his visit, and eventually he slammed out leaving everyone a shaking, gibbering wreck.

It was cold the next morning, and hot water was not available for shaving, so it was a case of doing one's best with cold tap water in the yard behind. My strong beard was hardly touched by this cold razor, and no doubt it looked as if I had not shaved. We had breakfast, and started to clean up in preparation for the midday return of the RPs, including the coke stove, so there was no heat whilst this was being done.

Being cold, the police staff could not wait for us to leave before they started to try to light their fire. In doing this, they had paper, coke and wood scattered round the base, just after we had cleaned it nicely. I know you are already ahead of me, and you are ready for the next event. Yes, right at this critical moment, there was a visitor, the RSM. The first thing he did was gaze up into my face and say 'Have you shaved this morning, sergeant?' I said that I had, but he was not convinced. He also noticed the state of the stove and accused us of failing to clean up. He referred to other matters from the previous evening, and when he finally left, he told me that I was on 'open arrest'. This meant that I was going to be put on a charge, and that I could not leave the camp. I would be brought before the squadron leader on Monday morning, but meanwhile I had to complete my duties as regimental orderly sergeant.

I have no idea what the remainder of the guard thought, but I was left feeling that I had just been hit by a 90 mile per hour express train, worse than a quivering jelly.

It was far worse not knowing what I was to endure, or what the outcome might be, but other members of the mess did not appear over-optimistic as to the outcome. Was my career as a sergeant going to be one of the shortest on record?

As orderly sergeant, my duties included attending all parades, checking the mess halls at mealtimes, and a variety of other duties, long since forgotten. I shall never know how I got through the next few hours. I experienced emotions never known either before or since, and although I am not normally a person who turns to prayer for solutions with any great expectation, nevertheless I spent much of my time asking to be released from this frightening ordeal. Ignorance is bliss, runs the old adage, but I was totally without any idea what would happen, and to add to this, I was desperately tired from lack of proper sleep. Yet somehow I managed to complete my various duties, and by Sunday evening I was ready to hear the worst.

Monday morning arrived, and at the appointed time I paraded before the squadron leader. Ranks below mine would normally parade on a charge, minus their belt and hat, but as a senior NCO I was allowed to keep mine on. The RSM read out a list of charges which made me sound like the worst criminal ever, and I was allowed to respond to them, but instead of being awarded punishment as I had anticipated, the squadron leader merely said 'Remanded for CO's orders,' which meant I had to go through the whole thing again. I did not know at the time that the squadron leader was not empowered to give out punishment to a senior NCO, it had to go before the commanding officer. Of course, not knowing this to be the proper procedure, my heart had sunk into my best boots.

The corridor outside the CO's office was rather like Paddington Station in the rush hour. Apart from the RSM and myself there were the squadron leader, the adjutant, my wing officer Capt Hubbard, old Uncle Tom Cobley and all. We all marched in, filling the small office completely. Once more the list of charges were read out, and I did my best to justify my behaviour. The RSM was in full flow, and never missed one item from the charge sheet. My main defence was inexperience, which was of course true, but if I felt that I should have acted differently, I admitted the fact. I also agreed to having made some errors of judgement. The squadron leader, and Capt Hubbard were now asked for character references.

As far as I can recall, the squadron leader was quite complimentary, but it was Capt Hubbard who really made all the difference. He said that I was one of his best instructors, and that my behaviour was very good. He added that he could not afford to lose me from his teaching staff. Until that point, I imagine that the result of the hearing hung in the balance, but this seemed to impress the CO. He considered the matter for a few moments, looked up and said 'Admonished, march out.' I gathered that meant that I was being told off, but that nothing bad would go on my service record. It also meant that I kept my stripes.

Back out in the corridor, when the officers had departed, the RSM looked at me, and in the kindliest voice I ever heard him use, he said 'Keep your nose clean in future, and don't be such a bloody fool again.' What I was unaware of was the fact that he had told the sergeants' mess caterer that there was likely to be 'one less for lunch'. He had, however made his point, shown that no-one could take any kind of liberty with him, and proved that he had no time for National Service senior NCOs.

I would never again want to go through such a traumatic experience, and was so relieved to return to normal. I gradually caught up with my lost sleep, and concentrated on my current squad of trainees.

One story which illustrates the matter of prisoners trying to escape from custody was told to me by former C Squadron stores corporal, Cyril Burford, with whom I recently had a pleasant meeting. Apparently he was on duty one cold dark night when one of the prisoners asked to use the toilet. Now toilets and washing basins were in an open yard at the rear of the guardroom, barbed wire spread round all four sides, but otherwise open to the elements. Cyril took this chap to the yard, and then went back inside to wait. Five minutes passed; the boots were still visible under the door. Ten minutes, the same. After fifteen, Cyril thought he had better check inside the cubicle. The boots were still there, but the prisoner, in just his pyjamas, had climbed over the barbed wire and disappeared. He was later caught in the middle of the moors, still wearing only nightware and socks. Two lucky escapes, the prisoner could easily have died from the cold, and Cyril could have faced a courts-martial for losing a prisoner. Cyril said, 'He must have been really desperate!'

Christmas was fast approaching. The mess had a grand raffle and all of us took part. I actually won a goose, although I had no idea where to keep it, or what I was going to do with it. Both questions were shortly to be answered. I was one of those who would be on duty over Christmas, and one of the married sergeants invited me to his home for Christmas Day. He had a refrigerator, and so I gave his wife the goose (in the purest sense of the word, that is). I cannot remember winning much in any raffle, before or since.

My parents were not overjoyed at the thought of my having to stay in Catterick at the festive season, but since there was only around three months' service still to complete, they accepted it, just as I had to. Amongst those going on leave was the sergeant who ran the mess bar, so I was detailed to take over from him. I think this had been deliberately organised because of my lack of real interest in drinking. The hours were very exacting, since the bar had to remain open until the last customer left, often well into the early hours, then stock had to be measured and counted, and I needed to re-open for the next lunch time. In addition I had to keep all takings under my bed until they could be banked. The worst part of the job was learning what mixes of drinks were meant by the various names, also how to serve them correctly. During that period, I believe my average time of going to bed was around 4.00 a.m. and I needed to rise again before 11.00.

I telephoned my parents several times, and found they were just having a quiet time, but at least I was kept busy, with little time to think about not being at home.

Promotion had set me aside from my corporal friends, although I soon got to know other sergeants in the mess living quarters. My favourite pastime was a game of billiards or snooker and although

I never became more than a lower than average player, it was enjoyable, and we had some laughs.

Despite my being left alone by the RSM after the incident, I realised that he was always watching, so took no chances.

Chapter Twelve

The Home Straight

One of my neighbours in the mess was a skilled electrician. He built himself a small television set with a screen around 6″ wide. There was a problem with reception, and his makeshift aerials were anything but efficient. What with the tiny size and the constant flickering, I declined his frequent invitations to go and view whatever programme he could discover. I doubt if the poor quality of picture can have done much for his eyesight.

Another neighbour was very 'camp'. There was a strong possibility that it was all an act, and I never really believed he was a full homosexual. His manner was much more that of a camp comic on the TV and never posed any problem. Of course, in those days to have been a practising homosexual would have been against Queen's Regulations (no pun intended!). Throughout my service, I never heard sex discussed in anything but a heterosexual manner, and there were even rumours that the army tea was laced with bromide to reduce sexual urges in the ranks. Of course, as a non tea-drinker, I was not aware of any effect, and kept my unsatisfied urges to myself.

Once everyone was back from Christmas leave, we were ready to resume normal life. I was awaiting another new intake to teach wireless to. However, this never happened. I was given a new and more responsible post, that of training potential instructors prior to them going down to Bovington. The pick of recent successful trainees from all the local training regiments of the Royal Armoured Corps were to complete a ten week cadre which was being held in our squadron. I had been chosen to train them.

It was of course an honour, and showed that they had great faith in my ability, but the one really great thing so far as I was concerned was that to do this job, I was excused all other duties. No more guards, no more orderly sergeant. I was about to enter the happiest period of my service, with responsibility to decide which of these men would be promoted and sent on to the big course, which I had completed barely a year before.

One activity I had enjoyed throughout my service was shooting on various rifle ranges, especially with the old Lee Enfield .303 rifle. My favourite distance was 500 yards, but I achieved fairly good results at either 100 or 1000 yards too. During training, we had also been given the opportunity to fire the Bren, the Sten and the .38 revolver, but the rifle was my favourite. I had received a 'first class shot' badge in the cadet force, but now I was to enjoy trying to get 'bulls' for real.

I took my new task very seriously, preparing each evening for the lessons I would give the following day.

I was really able to put into full practice all the important matters we had been taught whilst at Bovington; for example, working to the standard of the weakest pupil, and showing great patience. I am glad to say it was a happy class, and once they got used to starting to teach for themselves most of them became quite proficient at it. I think it would be wrong to describe them as natural teachers, since most people need coaching for the ability to emerge, but they responded well and quickly. The logistical side, all the wireless trucks, and the full range of equipment were available, together with the necessary drivers and ancilliary staff. The only thing that from time to time held up normal progress was the occasional flat battery, because someone had failed to ensure all of these items were charged each night. Everyone soon became aware that failure to ensure batteries being put on charge resulted in the individual being put on a charge instead!

Around this time, new radio sets were being introduced to the cavalry regiments, but fortunately for me they were still very much in experimental vogue. Otherwise it would have meant all current instructors being retaught too. These were the early transistor-operated sets, valves being considered old-fashioned. The new tank set would be the 52 set, but beyond that fact we knew little. I am not certain how long after my demob these new sets were in operation, or even if the two sets were used in tandem for any length of time.

I found it difficult to realise my time was nearing its end. When, as a new trooper, I began my training, the prospect of two years seemed daunting, but it had passed very swiftly, or at least most of it had.

At the start of the cadre I had less than three months to serve. Once again, I was sent for by the Commanding Officer, but I knew it was not for something I had done wrong – the Army had its own way of communicating that sort of news. Now it was to ask if I would consider signing on for another three years. Of course it was an honour, and a tribute to my abilities, and the carrot dangling before my nose was another promotion, this time to staff sergeant. Also it would be a paid position. He gave me a few days to make up my mind, and there was much to consider.

It would mean forgetting my civilian career, and that would then probably mean that I would need to make the army a career, and all that entailed. After those days of consideration, I decided that I would prefer to leave the service and resume my other career. It was a hard decision, and even today I am uncertain whether or not it was the right one. One thing is quite certain: my life would have been very different, and there have been times when I think it could have been for the best. Whatever choice one makes is based on what one sees at the time, and you have to learn to live with the consequences.

By this time, I had the subject right at my finger tips, although perhaps I had that niggling doubt as to whether or not I would find learning about new equipment difficult. I was teaching without reference to my comprehensive notes, and normally without reading the official manuals. The cadre was going well, so perhaps the other side of me was tempted to continue. I had the class in my best learning mode, and we had begun getting them to show their teaching abilities. We still went out on schemes to practise our various drills and use of equipment. The old couple were still ready with their beans on toast in their little back street cafe in Darlington, and my new class was also treated like members of their family. It could be cold on the north-east coast, bracing at Redcar, industrial at Middlesborough, and congested in Durham. I still managed to twist an occasional arm to get a drive, but in bad weather, I chickened out and left it to the B4 drivers.

My parents were talking of the possibility of driving up to Yorkshire to collect me when I was demobbed. I found a nice little hotel in Finkle Street, Richmond, which seemed to fit the bill. My day of release would also be my mother's birthday, so it could be celebrations all round. You may be interested to see the prices at that establishment in 1955, reproduced in Figure 1 below. Makes one realise how everything has inflated since that time!

The date would also coincide with the annual Admin inspection of the regiment but I did not have to be a part of either the parade or the inspection. Just keep out of the way, I was told.

A family bereavement, the death of my maternal grandfather, just a couple of weeks prior to the big day nearly made us alter our plans. However, the funeral took place, and our plans went ahead.

An ironic coincidence was also to take place on March 16th. RSM Blackshaw, who had been our scourge since his arrival, would be leaving the regiment and would be getting a commission in the Leicestershire Yeomanry. I would have given everything to be a fly on the wall when Albert (yes, he had a name) arrived at his new posting, particularly to see if he was capable of behaving like an officer and a gentleman, rather than a bullying sergeant major.

During the final days of the course, I had to decide which members were good enough to receive a stripe, and proceed to Bovington for their ten weeks hard work. I cannot remember if I failed anyone, or if they all passed. By the law of averages, I must

THE BLACK LION HOTEL	TARIFF
Telephone : Richmond 3121	★

Bed and Breakfast	16/6
Luncheon (Coffee extra)	4/6
Afternoon Tea	2/6
Dinner	6/–
Daily Rate (If claimed when room is booked, minimum of three days) ...	25/–
Weekly Terms	£7 7s.
Lock-up Garage (if available)	1/6
Extras (Early Morning Tea 7.45 a.m.) ...	6d.

"THE SMALL HOTEL IN THE SIDE STREET"

FINKLE STREET

RICHMOND · YORKS

FULLY LICENSED   RESIDENTIAL

Times of Meals:
Breakfast 8 to 9.15 a.m.
Lunch 12.30 to 1.45 p.m.
Afternoon Tea 3.30 to 5.30 p.m.
High Tea 4 to 6 p.m.
Dinner 7 to 7.45 p.m.

Figure 1   Hotel tariff, 1955.

say it would be more likely that some did not make it, but on that subject, my mind is a complete blank. Certainly they had all tried hard and given of their best, and you could not ask for more. I wrote my final reports, and we completed the training schedule with at least one day to spare. We still went into the classroom, and as I was within hours of leaving, I treated them to an impromptu show of how not to teach. Fooling around, I had the class in stitches. I dropped things deliberately, and made a farce out of picking them up. I think the light relief went down well with everyone.

The class dispersed to their next duties. I was packed and ready, with bedding and other not needed items safely back in the stores. However, I would need my uniform and basic equipment for the forthcoming TA duties, and I would not be allowed to leave until I had my release documents and my final pay, and it would be late morning before those were handed out. The inspection was taking place, and my dodging from hut to hut after the officers had visited was rather like an Aldwych farce. Hiding behind walls and bushes I managed to avoid being seen, until it was time to leave.

My parents drove to the regimental HQ offices, where I was waiting, and with me at the wheel of the car we headed for the A1 and Wetherby, where we planned to have lunch. I treated Mum and Dad out of the cash which had been saved for me over the two years, and was now a useful sum.

On the early part of the journey south there were patches of snow lying here and there, but it was a happy journey and I kept my parents amused telling them some of the things which had happened during the recent months. I still had to complete five years in the Queen's Own Worcestershire Hussars, based in Kidderminster, but the main part of the training was to be two weeks annual camp.

Chapter Thirteen

Out of the Frying Pan

My return to civilian life was but a few hours old when Kidderminster experienced one of the worst floods in living memory. The River Stour, which normally flowed peacefully past our shop, added to by a combination of heavy rain and melting snow, rose swiftly and without proper warning being given. I had just begun to work there again, and one of the first things I had to deal with was five feet of river water in the shop, leaving two feet of brown, stinking mud containing numerous stationery products from the shelves. It took several days to get the premises back to normal, and much hard work. So any idea I might have had of taking things easy for a while was swiftly squashed. By the summer it was almost forgotten, and I was able to go to the TA camp without worrying about the shop.

The camp was to be held in August at Tilshead on Salisbury Plain, a well-known training area. Most of the group travelled by public transport, but my mate Jerry (he who lost his stripes over going to the Windmill) had a little car, and offered to transport me and my equipment. One of the advantages of this move was that we had longer at home before having to set out, and we still arrived first.

Members of the Queen's Own Worcestershire Hussars also travelled from other depots, including Rubery, so it was quite a

111

large contingent that arrived at Tilshead and grabbed spaces in the tents

Jerry and I, being in the Wireless wing issuing and checking equipment, slept in the tents close to the administrative offices and the Naafi.

It was a burning hot August, with dust kicking up from every movement of the tracked vehicles, and from those which had tyres. Once or twice it was necessary to travel out to various locations with spares or replacements, my first experience of travelling in a half-track, and I can still remember the sore ribs which came about from speeding over uneven ground.

Most evenings we spent in the Naafi, having a sing-song and a pint or two, and we got to know several lads who had been demobbed before ourselves, an age spread of some two or three years. Guard rotas were set up, and although the same discipline was maintained, somehow there seemed to be more relaxation than at Catterick.

The main tented part of the camp was on a downward facing slope with the vehicle park just above. Our wing and the offices were off to one side and we slept in the wireless wing store to prevent any possible theft. At the end of each day, unless night exercises were scheduled, all tanks, together with other vehicles were parked in the vehicle park where the guards could keep them under observation. They were different tanks from the ones we had in Catterick, not Centurions, but either Charioteers or Comets.

Still on the secret list, these tanks were having their capabilities tested, but the brakes on them were metal and subject to expansion and contraction. Orders stated that all vehicles must be parked 'in gear' with handbrakes applied. August 17th was particularly hot, but as the night progressed, the air cooled and the metal contracted. One of the tanks, facing down towards the tents had not been left in gear, and in the comparative coolness of the early morning of August 18th the brake slipped and the tank began to roll downhill. At least two guards heard the noise, saw the vehicle move, and tried to give warnings with their whistles. The runaway hit two more tanks, also apparently not in gear, and these rolled onward and through several tents. By a miracle, several of the occupants were on guard, otherwise the carnage might well have been terrible. As it was, three chaps were killed outright and two more died either on the way to, or in, hospital.

The camp was in uproar, ambulances carried the victims away, and we discovered that one of the dead, at least, had been one of the regulars at the nightly Naafi shindigs, and thus a good pal. The news reached Midland Newspapers by midday, also the radio, and every local telephone was in permanent use with the survivors telling their relatives that they were all right. My memory now differs from at least one other person. I seemed to remember that we were soon sent home, and camp cancelled, but Gordon Pallett, a former member of the 67th Training Regiment, wearing the badges of the 11th Hussars (The Cherry Pickers), told me he attended one of the funerals. He thinks some stayed on in camp.

Gordon was driver and batman to Major Jewell, one of the senior officers. I trust his memory because he was more directly involved, and he had a very lucky escape indeed. He told his experience as follows.

'When I arrived in camp, I selected a space in my allotted tent, but shortly afterwards this other chap asked if he could have the bedspace instead of me. I saw no reason not to agree, but he was one of those hit by the runaway tank, being killed almost immediately. I remember waking during the night and hearing the squeak and rattle of tank tracks nearby, and before I knew what was happening, the canvas of the tent was ripped aside, and I could see the stars where previously there had been a cover.'

He tried to help the wounded by wrapping them in warm blankets after their severe shock. He told me that most of the others remained calm and did what they could. Only one person was unable to cope.

It seems that military discipline paid off during that incident.

There were inquests and a court of enquiry where a variety of possible causes were aired, but no blame was ever alloted and the reason for coincidental failure of different mechanical parts was not discovered.

The one thing which certainly was at fault was the decision to park heavy vehicles on a slope, facing down towards a tented camp. Very shortly afterwards, a huge ramp of earth was constructed between camp and vehicle park, and vehicles were then parked sideways.

I have read many reports of the incident, to try to see if any clear picture of responsibility emerges, but without success. To raise the issues again after nearly fifty years seems pointless, and only calculated to cause more pain, therefore I leave the known facts to speak for themselves, without comment.

It was my first, and last, camp. Later in the year the rule whereby we should complete five years in the TA was repealed, so that was the end of my military career, and brings me almost to the end of my book.

Chapter Fourteen

Catterick and Bovington Revisited

As I write this, we are in a new century, and fifty years further on. Those of us who have survived the intervening years and numerous careers are beyond middle age. In fact we are the grandparent generation. Our memories are most probably less reliable than they were, so I decided two things were needed. First, to try to contact those who had many of the same experiences, and then to revisit the two main camps involved.

The most changed of the two is Catterick. It is no longer the sprawling bustling camp of thirty thousand troops, and gone too are many of the amenities which were necessary to keep us out of mischief in our off-duty periods. The old railway links of Richmond and Camp Centre are long gone; it is difficult to see where the lines ran. In place of stations, buildings have sprung up, and what was the main barrack square of the 65th training regiment is now a block of accommodation for married families. Army vehicles are still in evidence, but to a lesser degree.

The original railway routes to the North East have changed. Trains no longer call at Rotherham or Pontefract; instead it is either Sheffield and Doncaster, or Leeds and Wakefield. The heavily industrial and steel region around Sheffield is now either empty, or has vandalised buildings, or areas of rubble. The line from King's Cross seems to be the same, but not from Birmingham. One of the few places which look almost unchanged from a distance, until you arrive, is York station with its glass canopied roof, but the platform arrangements are different.

If you were to be dropped by parachute into Darlington, you would be hard pressed to recognise it for the metropolis it was. That is of little surprise: most towns and cities have been altered beyond recognition.

Richmond remains a quiet little market town, unspoilt by progress, but buildings have been changed.

On the other hand, Bovington, though changed greatly and its security tightened considerably, is still recognisable. There are high barbed wire topped fences, a guardroom which is run in a very

The car park at Bovington, 2002 (formerly the parade ground for Wireless Wing).

secure manner, and it is identified clearly as the headquarters of the Royal Armoured Corps.

The huts where we lived for ten weeks are now storage units, the Tank Museum has been extended, and the public access and car park goes partly over where we used to parade. The Wireless Wing itself is further up the road, the garrison cinema has long gone and there are still plenty of sports facilities.

I was disappointed with the extended museum. Although there are many new exhibits, there is less about the history and insignia of the former cavalry regiments, many of them now merged together.

The training grounds can be hired at weekends for people wanting to drive a tank, under proper supervision I might add. Lawrence's cottage at Clouds Hill links with the old Tank Corps, and is rather sad and ironic at a period in history when we seem to have fallen out with the Arabs, who worshipped him as leader.

Oh well, such is life! The trips were worth making, as I remembered some things I had forgotten. After contacting others who served in the forces during the era I have recalled in these pages, I have realised that my memory is not all I thought it was, so where there are gaps or mistaken memories, I trust I may be forgiven. It has, however, been a genuine attempt to recall two years of military service.